Fortress • 59

Crusader Castles in Cyprus, Greece and the Aegean 1191–1571

David Nicolle • Illustrated by Adam Hook

Series editors Marcus Cowper and Nikolai Bogdanovic

First published in 2007 by Osprey Publishing

Midland House, West Way, Botley, Oxford OX2 0PH, UK

443 Park Avenue South, New York, NY 10016, USA

E-mail: info@ospreypublishing.com

ISBN 978 1 84176 976 9

Design: Ken Vail Graphic Design, Cambridge, UK

Typeset in Monotype Gill Sans and ITC Stone Serif

Cartography: Map Studio, Romsey, UK

Index by Alison Worthington

Originated by United Graphics, Singapore

Printed in China through Bookbuilders

07 08 09 10 11   10 9 8 7 6 5 4 3 2 1

A CIP catalogue record for this book is available from the British Library.

FOR A CATALOGUE OF ALL BOOKS PUBLISHED BY OSPREY MILITARY AND AVIATION PLEASE CONTACT:

Osprey Direct, c/o Random House Distribution Center, 400 Hahn Road, Westminster, MD 21157

Email: info@ospreydirect.com

Osprey Direct UK, P.O. Box 140, Wellingborough, Northants, NN8 2FA, UK

E-mail: info@ospreydirect.co.uk

www.ospreypublishing.com

Dedication

For Ian, Marian, Peter and Louise.

Artist's note

Readers may care to note that the original paintings from which the colour plates in this book were prepared are available for private sale. All reproduction copyright whatsoever is retained by the Publishers. All enquiries should be addressed to:

Scorpio Gallery
PO Box 475
Hailsham
East Sussex
BN27 2SL
UK

The Publishers regret that they can enter into no correspondence upon this matter.

The Fortress Study Group (FSG)

The object of the FSG is to advance the education of the public in the study of all aspects of fortifications and their armaments, especially works constructed to mount or resist artillery. The FSG holds an annual conference in September over a long weekend with visits and evening lectures, an annual tour abroad lasting about eight days, and an annual Members' Day.
The FSG journal *FORT* is published annually, and its newsletter *Casemate* is published three times a year. Membership is international. For further details, please contact:

The Secretary, c/o 6 Lanark Place, London, W9 1BS, UK

Contents

Introduction

The fortifications erected, repaired or reused by the Crusader States in Cyprus and around the Aegean have attracted less interest than those in and around the Holy Land. While the military and political situations which they reflected were also more complex than those in the Middle East, several of the states established by so-called Crusaders in Cyprus and Greece survived much longer than did the Crusader States on the Middle Eastern mainland. Others created in what are now north-western Turkey, Bulgaria, Macedonia, and Albania proved more ephemeral.

The Latin or Catholic Kingdom of Cyprus was established during the course of the Third Crusade, as a consequence of King Richard of England's unprovoked invasion of what was at the time a rebel-held Byzantine island. This was not the first invasion of the Orthodox Christian Byzantine empire by a Catholic western European army, but it was the first significant diversion of a major crusade that had set out to attack Islamic territory. The Fourth Crusade, sometimes described as 'The Great Betrayal', was the most famous such diversion, resulting in the heartlands of the Byzantine empire being temporarily replaced by a Catholic Christian or Latin 'Empire of Romania'. This, and its subsidiary Kingdom of Thessalonika, was very short-lived, but two other subsidiary states in central and southern Greece endured for centuries and left an architectural legacy in a land better known for ancient Greek and Roman remains.

Equally important were the widespread colonial outposts planted by the two greatest maritime republics of Italy on the coasts of what had been the Byzantine empire. First came Venice, whose ships transported the Fourth Crusade to the walls of the Byzantine capital of Constantinople, now named Istanbul. Next came Venice's rival Genoa, largely as an ally of the Byzantines as they fought back against the invading Crusaders. In fact the last western outposts to fall to the Ottoman Turkish empire – which conquered the mosaic of Orthodox or Catholic Christian and Islamic territories resulting from the Fourth Crusade – were Genoese and Venetian.

OPPOSITE PAGE Crusader and other western European fortifications in Greece and the Aegean (frontiers c.1360). Note that not all the High and Late Medieval fortifications of Greece and Aegean Turkey appear on this map. Medieval European names, where known, are given in brackets.

RIGHT The embrasures in the outer wall of the Crusader citadel at Mistra loom above the later Palace of the Byzantine Despots. (Author's photograph)

4

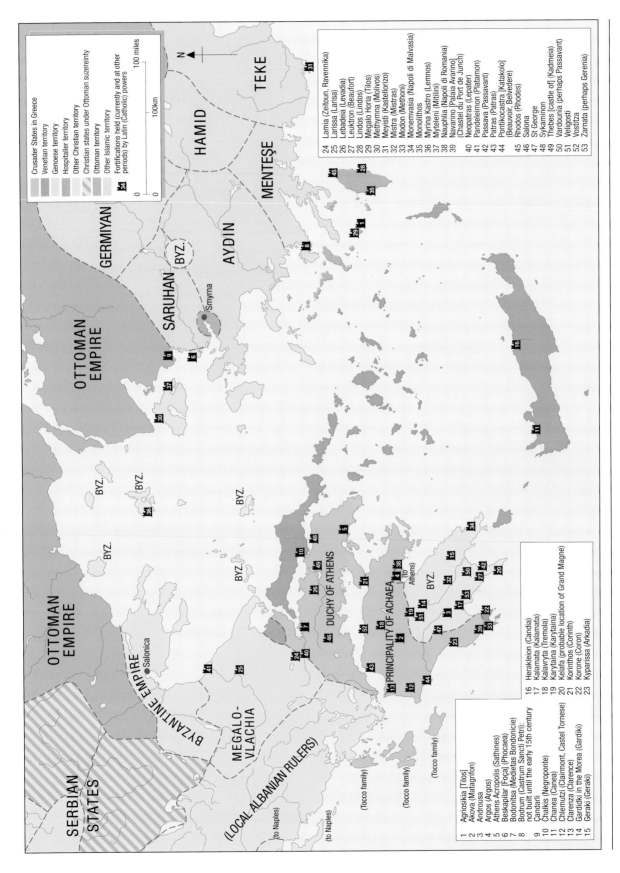

Crusader States in Greece
Venetian territory
Genoese territory
Hospitaller territory
Other Christian territory
Christian states under Ottoman suzereinty
Ottoman territory
Other Islamic territory
Fortifications held (currently and at other periods) by Latin (Catholic) powers

100 miles
100km

24 Lamia (Zeitoun, Ravennika)
25 Larissa (Larisa)
26 Lebadeia (Levadia)
27 Leuktron (Beaufort)
28 Lindos (Lindos)
29 Megalo Horia (Tilos)
30 Methymna (Molivos)
31 Meyisti (Kastellorizo)
32 Mistra (Mistras)
33 Modon (Methoni)
34 Monemvasia (Napoli di Malvasia)
35 Monolithos
36 Myrina Kastro (Lemnos)
37 Myteleni (Mitilini)
38 Nauphlia (Napoli di Romania)
39 Navarino [Palaia Avarino]
    (Chastel du Port de Junch)
40 Neopatras (Lepater)
41 Pandeleimon (Platamon)
42 Passava (Passavant)
43 Patras (Patras)
44 Pontikocastra [Katakolo]
    (Beauvoir, Belvedere)
45 Rhodos (Rhodes)
46 Salona
47 St George
48 Sykaminon
49 Thebes (castle of (Kadmeia)
50 Vardounia (perhaps Passavant)
51 Veligosti
52 Vostitza
53 Zarnata (perhaps Gerenia)

16 Herakleion (Candia)
17 Kalamata (Kalamata)
18 Kalavryta (Tremola)
19 Karytaina (Karytaina)
20 Kelafa (probable location of Grand Magne)
21 Korinthos (Corinth)
22 Korone (Coron)
23 Kyparissa (Arkadia)

1 Agriosikia [Tilos]
2 Akova (Matagrifon)
3 Androusa
4 Argos (Argos)
5 Athens Acropolis (Sathines)
6 Beskaplar [Foça] (Phocaea)
7 Bodonitsa (Medietas Bondonicie)
8 Bodrum (Castrum Sancti Petri:
  not built until the early 15th century
9 Candarli
10 Chalkis (Negroponte)
11 Chanea (Canea)
12 Chlemutzi (Clairmont, Castel Tornese)
13 Clarenza (Clarence)
14 Gardidiki in the Morea (Gardiki)
15 Geraki (Geraki)

5

The military circumstances of 'Crusader' fortifications in these regions differed significantly from those in and around the Holy Land, yet certain factors remained similar. Most historians highlight Italian naval dominance as being a key strategic consideration. However, as the Christians' naval superiority is too often overstated in relation to the Middle Eastern Crusader States, so the Christians' domination of the Aegean and Black seas well into the 15th century is similarly exaggerated. Turkish Islamic fleets could rarely challenge Italian or Crusader fleets until the rise of Ottoman naval power in the later 15th century and rarely attempted to do so. Instead pre-Ottoman Turkish, Mamluk (Syrian-Egyptian) and early Ottoman warships used their numerous and almost invariably smaller ships to raid Christian-held islands and coasts while the more powerful but less numerous Italian or Crusader warships were elsewhere. This had a profound impact upon the location, supply, defence, and garrisoning of 'Crusader' fortifications in these regions. Small forces put ashore by Muslim so-called 'pirates' sometimes penetrated deep inland, having an impact upon the internal as well as the coastal fortifications of the Crusader States and those of the larger Italian colonies.

Other geo-political factors are also widely misunderstood. After the fall of the remnants of the Byzantine empire to the Ottoman Turks in the 15th century, the preceding Byzantine decline came to be seen as inexorable. In reality, Byzantine successes in the early 14th century had made it seem possible that the empire would rebuild a substantial power base in the southern Balkans and Greece, while largely abandoning its previous Asian power base in Anatolia. For the Crusader States in Greece the essentially Orthodox Byzantine empire appeared a mortal threat, and was viewed as a serious regional rival by the Catholic rulers of southern Italy and Sicily. In the event this Byzantine revival faded after the Ottoman Turks established a European foothold on the Gallipoli peninsula. From there the Ottoman state expanded into the Balkans and Greece, becoming the greatest threat not only to the rump Byzantine empire, other Orthodox Christian states in the Balkans and the Crusader States in Greece, but also to Venetian and Genoese colonial outposts. This Ottoman expansion was carefully planned and steadily executed, completely altering the strategic situation faced by the remaining Crusader States and the Italian mercantile outposts.

The citadel of Lindos was the second most important fortress on the Hospitaller-ruled island of Rhodes. (Author's photograph)

Chronology

1191	Byzantine Cyprus conquered by King Richard I of England.
1194	Amaury of Lusignan becomes ruler of Cyprus; the following year he is recognized as a king (creation of the Crusader Kingdom of Cyprus).
1198	Proclamation of the Fourth Crusade.
1204	Fourth Crusade conquers the Byzantine imperial capital (Constantinople); Count Baldwin of Flanders elected as first Latin emperor.
1205	Conquest of Morea (Peloponnese, southern Greece) by Geoffrey de Villehardouin and William de Champlitte; establishment of the Crusader States in Greece.
1229–33	Civil war in Crusader Cyprus.
1235	John of Brienne saves Crusader Constantinople; defeat of Byzantines and Bulgarians.
1259	Crusader Principality of Achaea in Greece defeated by Byzantines at Pelagonia.
1261	Byzantine 'Emperor of Nicaea' retakes Crusader-ruled Constantinople; Crusader States also surrender Monemvasia, Mistra, and Maina in southern Greece.
1267	Crusader Principality of Achaea recognizes suzerainty of Charles of Anjou, ruler of southern Italy.
1271	Charles of Anjou recognized as king in Albania.
1278	Death of Prince William of Achaea; Charles of Anjou takes over direct government of Achaea.
1282	'Sicilian Vespers' revolt in Sicily against Charles of Anjou; Peter of Aragon invades Sicily.
1285	Death of Charles of Anjou; end of Angevin attempts to create an empire in Italy, Sicily, Greece, and the Crusader Kingdom of Jerusalem.
1291	Mamluks conquer Acre; end of the Kingdom of Jerusalem, though the title 'King of Jerusalem' remains, usually held by the Lusignan rulers of Cyprus.
1306	Crusader Order of the Hospitallers invades the Byzantine island of Rhodes.
1309	Hospitallers transfer their headquarters to Rhodes.
1311	Crusader forces in Greece defeated by the freebooting Catalan Company (mercenary army); Catalans take control of Athens and Thebes.
1313–16	Civil war in the Principality of Achaea; Ferdinand of Majorca, leader of the Catalan Company and claimant to Achaea, defeated and killed by Louis of Burgundy, grandson-in-law of William de Villehardouin.
1332	Agreement between Venice, the Hospitallers, and the Byzantine empire leads to formation of the first 'Crusade League' against the Turks (France and the Papacy join the following year).
1334	The Crusade League fleet defeats the Turks in the Gulf of Edremit.
1344	The Crusade League takes Smyrna (Izmir) from the Turks.
1346	The Genoese take over Chios and Foça from the Byzantines.
1354	Byzantines cede Lesbos to the Genoese; Ottomans seize a European bridgehead at Gallipoli.
1359	Peter I becomes king of Cyprus; Crusade League fleet defeats Turks at Lampacus.
1360–61	Kingdom of Cyprus occupies Corycos and Adalia on the southern coast of Anatolia.
1365	Crusade led by Peter I of Cyprus briefly occupies Alexandria (Egypt).

7

1366	Crusade led by Amadeus of Savoy in Thrace and Bulgaria.
1367	Peter I of Cyprus raids Cilicia and Syria.
1369	Assassination of Peter I of Cyprus; Genoese take control of Famagusta in Cyprus, expelling their Venetian rivals.
1371	Ottoman victory at the battle of Maritsa, followed by Ottoman conquest of most of Bulgaria and Macedonia.
1373–74	War between Cyprus and Genoa; Hospitallers take over the defence of Crusader-held Smyrna (Izmir).
1376	Principality of Achaea leased to the Hospitallers, but is taken over by the Navarrese Company (a mercenary army).
1378	The Hospitaller Grand Master is captured by the Ottomans at Arta in Greece.
1379	Navarrese Company takes control of Thebes.
1388	End of Catalan rule in Athens.
1389	Ottoman victory at the first battle of Kosova (Kosovo Field) leaves them as the dominant power in the Balkans.
1396	Large Crusading army destroyed by the Ottomans at the battle of Nicopolis.
1402	Timur-i Lenk (Tamerlane) conquers Izmir from the Hospitallers.
1406–07	Hospitallers start building a castle at Bodrum on the Anatolian mainland.
1424–25	Mamluks raid Cyprus and capture King Janus.
1432	Thomas Palaeologus, Byzantine despot of the Morea, takes the 'Crusader' Principality of Achaea.
1444	Mamluks unsuccessfully besiege Hospitaller Rhodes; Ottomans defeat a Crusader army at Varna.
1448	Ottomans defeat Hungarians at the second battle of Kosova.
1453	Ottomans conquer Constantinople; end of the Byzantine empire except for rival Byzantine states, which survive a few more years.
1456	Ottomans take Athens.
1457	A papal fleet raids the Aegean and occupies Samothrace, Thasos, and Lemnos.
1458	James 'the Archbishop' becomes king of Cyprus with help from the Mamluk Sultan.
1462	Ottomans conquer Genoese Lesbos.
1470	Ottomans conquer Venetian Euboea.
1472	Crusade League attacks Turkish Antalya and Izmir.
1473	Catherine Cornara, a Venetian noblewoman, becomes regent of Cyprus following the death of her husband King James, and is proclaimed queen the following year.
1480	Unsuccessful Ottoman siege of Hospitaller-ruled Rhodes; Ottoman forces occupy Otranto in southern Italy for a year.
1489	Queen Catherine abdicates and hands the island of Cyprus over to the Venetian Republic.
1516	Ottomans conquer the Mamluk Sultanate in Syria and Egypt.
1522	Ottomans conquer Hospitaller-ruled Rhodes.
1570–73	Ottomans conquer Venetian-ruled Cyprus.

Design and development

The Crusaders who conquered so much Byzantine territory also seized a variety of fortifications. These they mostly reused and strengthened. Cyprus, despite its seemingly exposed situation in the eastern Mediterranean, had not been strongly fortified by the Byzantines and the important town of Famagusta had only minor defences. The Crusaders now added more, strengthening Famagusta's two or three gates and constructing a tower to control the harbour entrance. Under Lusignan rule there were four types of fortification in Cyprus: isolated mountain-top castles in the north of the island, such as Buffavento, St Hilarion, and Kantara; coastal towns with citadels, such as Paphos, Limassol, and Magusa; inland towns with minimal defences, such as Nicosia; and small rural castles.

In the early Crusader period the towns did not apparently have properly defensible curtain walls. European naval superiority and the relative poverty of the Lusignan kingdom might also account for the majority of Cypriot fortifications being old fashioned, with barrel vaulting rather than the ribbed vaulting already seen in many Crusader castles in Syria. This traditionalism continued in the 14th century, despite the increased external threats following the fall of the mainland Crusader states, and instead of being replaced by modern fortifications, the large tower-type castles of Lusignan Cyprus were merely strengthened. Only in the mid 15th century were new fortifications built to face the new threat from gunpowder artillery, often enveloping rather than replacing the earlier structures.

Inside one of the massive vaulted chambers of the donjon of Chlemutzi (Clairmont) castle. This space would have been divided into two floors. (Ian Meigh)

One Cypriot castle did not, however, fit this pattern. Although the 'Castle of Forty Columns' at Paphos is generally believed to have been a new Crusader fortress dating from the very early 13th century, it has also been suggested that the inner enceinte is Byzantine, dating from the late 7th and 8th centuries. Others suggest that a donjon was built immediately after the Crusader conquest, but was replaced by the distinctive concentric castle whose ruins exist today. Attention has also been drawn to the similarities between the castle at Paphos and the earlier concentric castle of Belvoir in Palestine (see Fortress 21: *Crusader Castles in the Holy Land 1097–1192*), which was built by the Hospitallers. Paphos may also have a connection with the Hospitallers, who helped defend the new Crusader outpost in 1198. The Castle of Forty Columns remained the only one of its type in Cyprus and, following the Fourth Crusade's conquest of Constantinople in 1204, may have been considered redundant. Although construction was almost complete, work ceased when the site was hit by an earthquake.

The early Crusader rulers of Cyprus did strengthen several coastal towns in the 13th century. At Kyrenia the Lusignans rebuilt the northern and eastern sea-facing walls of a Byzantine fort while new walls were added to the landward sides, each containing a *chemin de ronde* connecting arrow-slits. This Lusignan fortress probably had corner towers, though only one D-shaped example survives. Royal apartments on the west side

The Frankish tower at Markopoulo, north-east of Athens. It is one of the best preserved free-standing towers on the Greek mainland. (P. Lock)

perhaps strengthened the castle entrance and there was a chapel over the inner gate.

A castle had been constructed at Limassol by 1228, perhaps including the French-style, square, two-storey keep in the centre of town, which is now encased in 14th–15th-century fortifications. It was a small but interesting structure with simple wooden floors in its upper levels. The citadel at Magusa (Famagusta) largely dates from after the loss of the Crusaders' remaining mainland enclaves in 1291, but might incorporate the 'sea tower' mentioned during Emperor Frederick II's Crusade. The coastal flank of Magusa was defended by a rectangular castle with corner towers built before 1310. From there a chain could close the harbour entrance. By the early 15th century the town defences consisted of a roughly rectangular walled enclosure with at least 15 regularly spaced towers, plus smaller turrets. In 1441 the Genoese added a small fort, the Gripparia, defending a secondary entrance into the port. The sea wall was pierced by a marine gate close to the Comerc mercantile area and an arsenal gate, which could be walled up in an emergency. However, Magusa had few land gates, the main one being the strongly fortified Limassol Gate, which also included a substantial *bretéche*.

Several Crusader castles in the mountains of northern Cyprus made use of existing Byzantine fortifications, while the new lowland castles were much less dramatic. The Hospitaller keep at Kolossi is neither powerful nor sophisticated, although it was sufficient to dominate its rural surroundings and serve as an administrative centre. Similarly, the 13th-century fortifications of the inland city of Nicosia consisted only of a citadel, city walls not being added until the 14th century.

The situation was different in regions closer to Constantinople. Here the existing Byzantine defences were very strong. Nevertheless, the fortifications of Izmit (Nicomedia) had recently been damaged by earthquake and the Crusader occupiers apparently did some limited repair work.

In Greece itself the majority of Crusader fortifications were based upon Byzantine or earlier defences, but this had been a backwater, far from the most threatened frontiers of the Byzantine empire, and most of the fortifications were simple. Virtually all were reused by the Crusader conquerors, though it is often difficult to identify precisely when. In other places the newly arrived Westerners built castles on new sites such as Veligosti, Geraki, Kalavryta, Karytaina, the lower peaks of Corinth, Mistra, Chlemutzi, Old Navarino, and Leuktron. Most of this work was done in the first 75 years, but other fortifications mentioned in the documentary sources have either disappeared or not yet been identified. Nevertheless it seems clear that the Crusaders preferred to strengthen what existed, as at the upper site at Corinth, Argos, Kyparissa, Nauphlia (Nafplion), Kalamata, Monemvasia and Patras. Here it is sometimes difficult to confirm whether the newcomers altered the basic plans of such fortifications. At Acrocorinth (upper Corinth) they merely added outworks and a powerful keep. At Patras the rectangular tower and courtyard of a Byzantine archbishop's palace required little to be transformed into a fortress. For example *The Chronicle of the Morea* stated that, at the time of its capture in 1210, Nauphlia already consisted of 'a castle in two enclosures'.

A study of surviving Crusader fortifications suggests that they were almost entirely defensive rather than offensive bases. Even so, most were lost to the Byzantines in the late 13th and early 14th centuries as a result of negotiation or treachery, very few falling to siege or direct assault. Despite the careful strategic location of key Crusader castles, they remained remarkably old-fashioned in design, reflecting what was, in military terms, a backwater of western European civilization. Apart from Clairmont (Chlemutzi), most were also built with limited materials, money and manpower.

The relative unimportance of castles is clear in the description of the *Parlement des Dames* held in the aftermath of a serious military defeat by the Byzantines. Commenting on how the captured Prince William of Achaea had offered to hand over the fortresses of Mistra, Monemvasia and Grand Maine in exchange for his release, Sir Pierre de Vaux, 'the wisest man in all the principality' and one of only two secular lords present, maintained:

> If the basileus [Byzantine emperor] takes these three castles, he will not hold to the oaths which he has sworn. He will send here against us many armies and troops that will throw us out of here and disinherit us. Therefore, that you may recognize my good faith, I say and affirm I will do this; I will enter prison and the prince, let him come out, or if it be a question of ransoming him for sums of hyperpyra [Byantine coins], I will pledge my land for denarii [another form of coinage], and thus let the ransom of my liege lord be paid.

Exterior of the east gate of Patras castle, as it appeared in 1938. The substantial machicolations above the entrance might date from after the Ottoman Turkish conquest. (A. Bon)

The Lord of Karytaina, who had been released by the Byzantines to act as an emissary, replied:

> The castle of Monemvasia, as everyone knows, was won by our lord, the prince, himself. Maina and Mistra were built by him, and it would be a sin and a great rebuke for him and his followers to die in prison for the sake of castles which he himself had won and built. Just let him escape the torment of the prison he is in, and afterwards God will help him to capture his castles and to have them as his own.[1]

The castles were handed over – but were never regained.

Crusader castles in Greece fall into clear categories, reflecting the geography of the country. For example, a steep cliff removed the need for anything more than a thin parapet wall on that side of the site, as at Acrocorinth, Nauphlia, Monemvasia, Kalamata, Arkadia, and Old Navarino. Here these 13th-century Greek castles were similar to several 12th-century Crusader castles in Syria and Lebanon. At Monemvasia the hilltop was almost entirely surrounded by cliffs, resulting in a curtain wall that followed the summit, plus a keep and enclosures to defend the few accessible slopes. A more distinctive feature of several Greek Crusader castles was the huge areas enclosed by their curtain walls. At Livadia in central Greece this was used for growing crops in the late 14th century. On the other hand large donjons were rarer than in western Europe or the Crusader Middle East.

Less is known about the organization, costs, and manpower of castle-building in Crusader Greece than in Crusader Syria. Most workers were locals and money was almost invariably short. Crusader repairs to the Byzantine fortifications of Izmit (Nicomedia) show no evidence of western European workmanship.

---

[1] Anon (tr. Lurier, H.E.) *The Chronicle of the Morea, Crusaders as Conquerors* (New York, 1964), 201.

Reconstruction of the 13th-century rural tower at Haliartos, Greece

The tower at Haliartos is one of the best-preserved examples of this type of isolated Crusader fortification, and enough survives to permit a reasonably reliable reconstruction. Although the masonry of the tower is quite crude, roughly rectangular ashlar blocks form the corners of the structure. The building had five levels, two of which were supported by vaulting (fourth and first – the vault at fourth level runs east–west while that at first level runs north–south) and two by timber beams (second and third levels). Rough wooden stairs or ladders linked each level. The fifth and topmost level (1) could be described as a fighting platform, and its crenellations are based upon those surviving on another tower. The fourth-level chamber is illuminated by the only large arched window (2) in the building. It is immediately above the entrance door (3), perhaps being used to drop missiles upon unwanted visitors. This rectangular entrance at the third level was closed by a wooden door, outside of which is a wooden platform supported by substantial beams thrust into put-log holes. Comparable beams support other external wooden structures. The narrower apertures that allow light into several levels (4) may also have served as arrow-slits; in the south walls these are only on the second and third levels but on the east and west walls there are also slits in the first level. The beams that support the flat ceilings and planked floors are thrust into sequences of holes along the insides of the walls and also rest on ledges. Based on the position of the put-log holes it seems that a central section of the access stairway might have been removable (5), like the lowest stairs or ladder (6). The first level probably served as a storage chamber. Floor plans for four of the levels are shown to the left of the main illustration.

Prisoners-of-war, both Muslim and fellow Christian, were often forced to work on castle-building; we know that Genoese prisoners were labouring at Nicosia in the late 14th century. On Hospitaller-ruled Rhodes, Greek peasants were obliged to take part in such work, while more skilled Greek masons had higher status and greater responsibility. By the mid 15th century such Master Wall Builders were exempt from military service and were given grain from the Order's own granary. Their high status also meant that they could form part of the committees that inspected castles throughout Hospitaller territory.

While Hospitaller island fortifications were often of the highest quality, Crusader defences on the Greek mainland and some other islands were mostly of very inferior construction, made from poor quality local limestone and soft (though easily cut) poros. Existing masonry was also used, as at Kalamata where the donjon and part of the inner enceinte seem to have been reconstructed from a derelict Byzantine fortress. Meanwhile there was widespread continuation of the Byzantine tradition of incorporating bands of thin bricks or tiles between layers of stonework. Ancient Greek or Roman masonry was sometimes used, though for structural rather than decorative reasons as seen at Salona in central Greece.

Part of the interior of the mountain-top upper citadel of the Dieudamour or St Hilarion castle in Cyprus. (Marion Youden).

Reconstruction of the 13th-century rural tower at Haliartos, Greece

Fourth level

Third level

Second level

First level

Continuity from the Byzantine past, limited western influence during the Crusader occupation, and comparable continuity into the Ottoman period, often make it difficult to date surviving masonry. Having to rely on local masons and even architects, the Crusaders seemed unable to build in the styles of their homelands, even if they wished. The normal result was a simplified, old-fashioned, late-Romanesque style with provincial Byzantine elements. The regular ashlar blocks favoured in Crusader Syria and Palestine were normally seen only in the corners and sometimes in vaults. Similarly, the way buildings were assembled generally reflected local traditions, and there seem to have been few differences between periods or patrons. Somewhat later at Clairmont (Chlemutzi) large, carefully cut poros blocks were used for gates, the angles of buildings, pilasters, and windows, while vaults were constructed from ashlar. Many structures consisted of rough limestone blocks and ceramic tiles set in hard mortar, or of mixed rubble walling; alternatively, as at Patras, Kyparissa, Kalamata and Nauphlia, virtually uncut 'fieldstones' were simply laid horizontally.

Although the Crusaders who conquered Greece in the early 13th century brought with them essentially French ideas of fortification, their successors generally adopted previous Byzantine styles while adding western European elements, resulting in a varied style of military architecture. Thereafter the main outside influence came from Italy, but a great age of Italian castle-building had actually ended in the mid 13th century. Until the 14th and 15th centuries the main Italian influence was in the design of water-storage facilities and, perhaps, upon those tall, isolated towers that characterized parts of the Greek Crusader states (see below). A new age of Italian originality emerged in the 14th and 15th centuries, with an emphasis on comfort, magnificence, and the resistance to gunpowder artillery.

Meanwhile the walls of Crusader castles in Greece remained vertical and as high as possible, with an occasional stepped talus at the base, until the later 14th century. After this, walls with a slightly sloped, or battered, outer face appeared, perhaps reflecting later Byzantine ideas. The only 13th-century parapets known to survive were at Chlemutzi, where the crenellations of the original keep were incorporated into a heightened wall, the merlons being square, without loopholes. The only evidence for an early machicolation has been found at Karytaina, other fortified walls being plain though a *bretéche* was sometimes added above the entrance.

Most towers were tall, rectangular, and projected forwards a short distance, but were generally little or no higher than the walls. Many were partially open at the rear or contained a vaulted chamber in their upper storey, as seen in the southern flank of the keep at Patras and part of the curtain wall of Acrocorinth.

The castle of Vardounia in southern Greece is a typical mountain-top castle with a curtain wall and major tower at the highest point. (P. Burridge)

A few half-round towers date from the early 13th century – the first to be used in Greece since antiquity – and are strikingly different from the stark squareness of Byzantine fortification.

The donjons of most 13th-century castles were almost square, that at Acrocorinth being built upon a characteristically French base with almost pyramid-like sides, while at Mistra and Clairmont a *chemin de ronde* runs round the top of the keep. Most entrances consisted of straight-through gates with wooden doors secured by horizontal beams, but portcullises were rare and barbicans almost unknown. Clairmont is again an exception, its outer gate originally being a rectangular building with a portcullis, set into a recess of the enceinte. Most early Crusader gates consisted of simple passages under a vault of arches, as in the east curtain wall of Clairmont, the keep of Acrocorinth, the inner redoubt of the Crusader castle at Mistra, and the east flank of the summit fort at Monemvasia. The distinctive hexagonal keep at Clairmont has a more elaborate entrance consisting of broad, inset archways in either face of an entrance chamber masking a tall, round-vaulted inner passage.

Clairmont also includes the greatest variety of early 13th-century windows, the most striking having a tall, wide opening like a passage, with a depressed vault of arches cut from poros stone into which a poros screen pierced with twin lancet windows is fitted. Although these castles date from the same period as the great Gothic structures of western Europe, pointed Gothic arches only appear at Clairmont, Karytaina, and in a few religious buildings.

Carved architectural decoration is extraordinarily rare in surviving Greek Crusader structures, and where it does exist it is old-fashioned and almost minimalist. The incorporation of ceramic tiles or thin bricks usually provided what little surface decoration there was. This was just one example of the mutual artistic influence between the Crusader States and the fragmented remnants of the Byzantine empire, which was felt more strongly on the mainland than on the Italian-ruled islands. The architectural historian Ramsay Traquair wrote of such artistic developments: 'The conquerors themselves must have become "Byzantinised" and the Gothic influence slowly wanes. Yet at intervals some more homeloving Frank would turn his thoughts westwards, and … import into his building the forms … from which he had come, or which his craftsmen knew best.' Yet this was much more apparent in the design and decoration of tombs than of buildings.[2]

Most Crusader fortifications in Greece have a village nearby, whereas several lowland towns declined or were even abandoned. Even more typical of Crusader-ruled regions in central if not southern Greece were numerous isolated towers. Few were sited for strategic reasons. Except on Venetian-ruled Euboea, most of these towers were not visible one from another and only a handful were associated with obvious settlements. Their purposes and date of construction remain a matter of debate, though the majority seem to have been constructed during a period of feudal fragmentation. Most were entered at first-floor level via a removable ladder, completely lack ornamentation, and were almost certainly built by local craftsmen. The lack of many loopholes, machicolations, or hoardings, and the minimal space for supplies, indicate that their military role was limited.

Surprisingly, given the wealth of their 'mother city' and their vital role as a chain of commercial outposts, the fortifications of the Venetian colonial empire were even more inferior in construction. Even at Methoni, which the Venetians retook after a brief Genoese occupation, their new urban defences consisted of small, square, open-backed towers linked by low walls around a peninsula, which was sealed at its northern end by a castle. Inside this walled area stood the town, its port, and a cathedral. Meanwhile, the Genoese remained the dominant western European commercial and naval power in the

[2] Traquair, R. 'Frankish Architecture in Greece', *Journal of the Royal Institute of British Architects*, 31 (1923/24) 86.

A machicolated tower at the south-eastern corner of the Genoese castle at Methymna (Molivos) on the island of Lesbos. (Author's photograph)

Black Sea. Here existing coastal fortifications reflected various cultures, the most important being the Byzantine. The military architecture of the rising states of Moldavia and Wallachia (today in Romania and Moldova) used the old Byzantine concept of a walled enclosure, or the traditional earth and timber fortifications of Hungary and the Balkans. During the later 13th and 14th centuries, however, western European influences reached the north-western coasts of the Black Sea via the Genoese colonial outposts, Hungary, and the short-lived Crusader 'Latin Empire of Constantinople'.

The most important Genoese colony was in fact Pera (now Galata), a suburb of Istanbul (Constantinople). Here on the northern side of the Golden Horn, the original Genoese colony was destroyed by its Venetian rivals in 1296. Seven years later the Byzantine authorities gave the Genoese a substantially larger area where they re-established a colony defended by a moat or ditch. In 1313 the *podestà* or local Genoese governor, Montano de Marini, built the first land wall around Pera. A sea wall was in place before 1324, after which the Genoese added towers to their land walls, the biggest of which, the Galata Tower, still dominates the skyline.

Elsewhere the Genoese seized substantial pieces of ground that they defended with long walls, though the areas enclosed were not necessarily then filled with buildings. The biggest of these Genoese outposts were established on or near the Crimean peninsula. Here Kaffa was strongly defended by land and sea walls, which, by 1352, were 718m long and incorporated numerous towers. Even this was considered inadequate and Genoa proposed strengthening the fortifications while increased reserves of food and weapons were stored inside the walled *commune*. The fortifications themselves were, however, still Byzantine-style plain walls with tall rectangular towers. Far to the south, on the Aegean island of Chios, a five-sided castrum was erected for the first Genoese rulers in 1346 – with three sides facing the Greek town, one facing the port, and the fifth facing the coast. According to a surviving contract written by the *Mahone* or local Genoese authorities in 1461, a master mason was to erect a wall 3.46m wide at its base and 2.97m wide at its summit.

The quality of Italian colonial fortifications, particularly those of the Venetians, improved markedly during the gunpowder revolution of the 15th century. Newly strengthened defences emerged as being amongst the most advanced anywhere. In fact the Venetians, who purchased Nauphlia in 1388, refortified it so thoroughly that little trace of previous Crusader construction can be seen. Similarly the new walls that the Venetians built around the promontory of Methoni were designed to resist cannon, while a moat was excavated across the landward side and a *fausse braie* was added in front of the land walls. The fortifications that the Venetians constructed in Cyprus after they took over the island in 1489 demolished many earlier defences and included some notably advanced military architecture, with massive, solid earth bastions in the Italian style, as seen at Magusa, Kyrenia and Limassol.

The principles of defence

Until the second half the 15th century the old principles of defence and attack dominated the western European outposts in Cyprus, Greece and the Black Sea. While the attackers aimed to get over a wall or to undermine it, the defenders largely relied on the height and thickness of their walls to resist – actively or passively. The increasingly effective stone-throwing siege machines in both attack and defence had their impact upon the design of towers, while the introduction of cannon at first merely speeded up the process of thickening the walls. Later on, however, the power of cannon led to the lowering of fortified walls and resulted in siege warfare involving less physical combat, though more intensive or prolonged bombardment. The excavation of siege entrenchments by besiegers as a defence against counter bombardment, and more sprawling outworks being added by defenders to fortifications to keep attackers at a distance, were also features of this period. The need to protect the flanks of a fortified place from bombardment similarly led to the construction of the strictly geometric fortifications that began to appear in Venetian Greek outposts in the very late 15th and early 16th centuries.

Until almost the end of the period under consideration, crossbows remained the most important anti-personnel weapons in the hands of those defending Crusader and other western fortifications. Crossbows also became vitally important in later Byzantine and local Balkan armies, and even to some extent in early Ottoman Turkish forces. The paramount defensive role of crossbows

The north-east wall and round northern tower of Androusa castle. (A. Bon)

was emphasized by Theodore Palaeologus in his 1326 military treatise, written in Greek but translated into Latin four years later. Its partially Byzantine author was an experienced soldier who was also marquis of Monferrat in early 14th-century Italy. However, little of his book dealt with siege warfare, perhaps reinforcing the impression that siege warfare remained relative unimportant in these regions.

Apart from in Cyprus, which was under constant threat from the Mamluk Sultanate, the Crusader occupiers often cut corners in the design and construction of their castles, especially on mountainous sites where natural geography was as important as man-made structures. Even where fortifications did exist, they were not necessarily defended. For example, in 1311, after the defeat of the local Crusader army by the mercenary Catalan Company, the citizens of Thebes surrendered without a struggle despite the fact that their castle was in good condition and its owner, Count Nicholas II, had survived the battle. In 1331 the Catalans themselves destroyed the castle of Thebes, rather than defending it and thus risking it falling intact into enemy hands. Indeed the castle seems to have been regarded more as a prize to be won or lost than as a strongpoint to be defended. Much the same was seen elsewhere during the early 14th-century struggle for domination in the Principality of Achaea. Castles remained symbols of authority or palaces, but in military terms the issue was decided elsewhere.

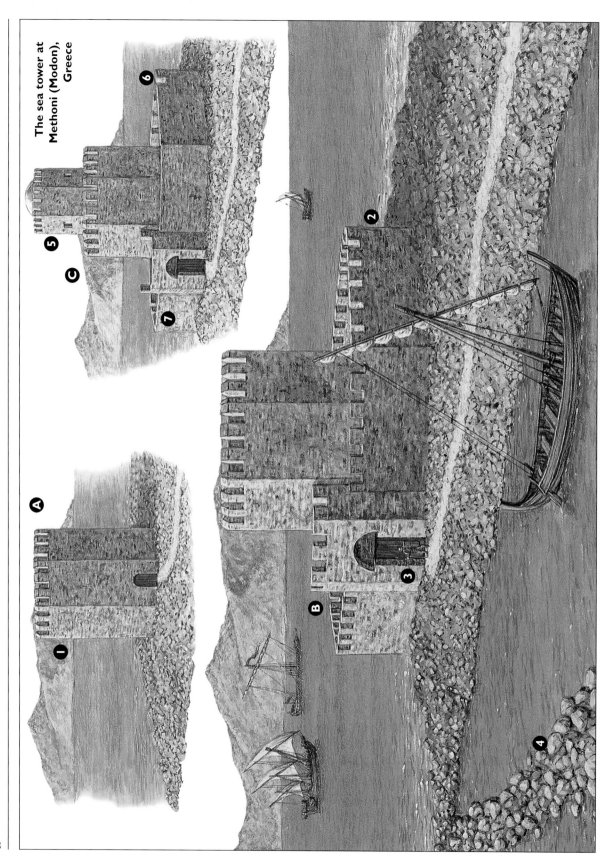

The sea tower at Methoni (Modon), Greece

The sea tower at Methoni (Modon), Greece

The small tower at the far end of the narrow peninsula upon which Methoni (Modon) was built was intended to guard the entrance to the harbour. From here the movement of shipping could be observed and an enemy could not threaten the fortified town from this direction. At its centre was an eight-sided *turris* or tower, which dated from before the Crusader conquest of southern Greece. It probably never had any embrasures or arrow-slits and was entered by a simple arched doorway. During this early period, and for more than a century and a half of western European occupation, the *turris* remained unchanged. Nor was there yet a man-made breakwater or mole to shelter the otherwise exposed anchorage on the eastern side of the peninsula. In 1387 the Venetians, who now controlled Methoni, added a lower, outer circuit wall. Above and to each side of the entrance, this wall was higher than elsewhere. A new breakwater was probably constructed around the same time, consisting of large stones dropped into the shallow water. Today the top of this shattered breakwater is beneath the waves, but it was presumably above sea level when originally constructed. A smaller eight-sided turret was added to the top of the original *turris* around 1500, though its dome might date from the late Venetian or early Ottoman Turkish occupation. Most of the embrasures in the previously crenellated outer wall were also removed or filled in at some unspecified date, especially on those sides overlooking the harbour. The wall above the entrance was similarly lowered. These alterations were almost certainly intended to make the little fort more suitable for firearms and light cannon.

Key

A The fortifications as they looked in the late 13th century.

B The fortifications as they looked at the end of the 14th century.

C The fortifications as they looked in the early 16th century.

1 The original eight-sided Byzantine or early Crusader *turris* (tower) before the addition of the outer defences. Note there was no breakwater at this date.

2 The new eight-sided outer wall constructed in 1387.

3 Outer gate with a partially inset, arched recess above the rectangular doorway.

4 Breakwater made of large stones.

5 Small eight-sided and domed turret added to the top of the original Byzantine or early Crusader *turris*.

6 The late 14th-century, eight-sided outer wall was modified by the Venetians for firearms and cannon around 1500.

7 Most of the embrasures in the previously crenellated outer wall were removed or filled in, especially on the sides overlooking the harbour. Some of this might have been repair-work by the Ottoman Turks after they captured the sea-tower at Methoni.

The small isolated towers that dotted the Duchy of Athens were even more obviously passive. Though few seem to have been associated with a significant settlement site, most were located in agricultural areas and presumably served as refuges for the local Latin elite. The role of fortified ports and small coastal enclaves is more obvious. Medieval Mediterranean navigation largely consisted of coastal routes and short hops between secure ports whose defences varied according to local circumstances. Old Navarino, built around 1278 by Nicholas II de St Omer, had upper and lower fortified enclosures without a strong donjon, presumably because Old Navarino was itself in such a dominating location. On the other hand the Galata Tower in Istanbul was designed as the key point in the defence of the walled colony of Pera. There seem, in fact, to have been major efforts to construct such central strong points from the late 14th century onwards. Several fortified coastal enclaves were characterized by

Bodrum castle with its tall keep and lower outworks, designed to house and to resist artillery, overlooking the harbour. (Author's photograph)

Top: a 14th-century bombard cannon from the island of Giurgiu in the lower Danube, probably Genoese. Bottom: a 15th-century bronze cannon, probably supplied to the Aq Qoyunlu ruler of eastern Turkey by Venice. (Archaeological Museum, Karaman)

having few gates through their land walls, but a larger number through their sea walls or those leading to their harbour. These outposts were, in effect, fortified markets and mostly consisted of a good port backed by a strong point on a high place, with a walled town developing between the two. Where there was no suitable highpoint to be fortified, a castle could be built next to the coast or the harbour.

At Methoni, in Greece, a small 'sea fort' on a rocky islet defended the mole, which gave additional shelter to the harbour. The role of its garrison was probably more to inhibit smugglers than to stand up to a serious assault. Crossbowmen based in the sea fort formed a first line of defence against any hostile naval attack, and the tower itself was octagonal to avoid blind spots. The size of the garrison is unknown, but probably included infantry to patrol the mole while crossbowmen defended the tower itself. A garrison on the nearby island of Sapientza could be isolated from the mainland by enemy shipping, so their role was probably only to defend Sapientza itself. There was no mention of a chain across the entrance to Methoni's harbour, but later, on the eve of the Ottoman conquest, Venetian records mention a project to 'narrow its entrance' by building a *porporella* or *argine*, a massive breakwater constructed in the same way as the mole. It was probably intended to run from the southern end of the sea fort towards Sapientza, to narrow the channel, but no remains have been found and the ambitious programme was probably never carried out.

The avoidance of surprise attacks was clearly important for isolated outposts. For this reason the Hospitallers established a chain of fire-beacons between the offshore islet of Castellorizo, Rhodes, and Kos. This must have involved otherwise unrecorded beacons on the Turkish mainland, as Castellorizo and Rhodes were too distant for direct line-of-sight. One of the main purposes of such beacons would have been to give Rhodes warning of any approaching Mamluk fleet, who were the main threat to the Hospitallers before the rise of the Ottomans in the mid 15th century. Large enemy fleets sailing from the eastern Mediterranean normally hugged the coasts and were thus visible from Castellorizo.

Mountain-top castles in Cyprus and Greece were similarly difficult to surprise. Their picturesque locations can sometimes appear puzzling; taking St Hilarion as an example, the castle's sheer northern flank falls approximately 500m, making the man-made defences seem somewhat superflous. On the other hand, the very inaccessibility of these locations meant that their garrisons could not easily swoop down on a foe below.

Coastal positions demonstrate the same concern to avoid surprise. Amasra on the Black Sea was a major Byzantine fortification before the Genoese established a colony in 1398. Here communication between the coast and the interior was very difficult because a sequence of steep coastal ranges runs parallel to the shore. Nevertheless, Amasra fell to the Ottomans 60 years later. Other Genoese outposts had fewer natural advantages and were more difficult to protect. The lines of Genoese defences normally followed those of the existing – usually Byzantine – fortifications, which mostly consisted of a single wall with widely spaced towers enclosing the town and port, often with a citadel at the highest point. Some of these urban walls were later extended to enclose new suburbs. Magusa, in Cyprus, was located on a low-lying coastal plain where there are no hills between the city and the interior. However, the coastal plain itself was infertile and unhealthy, thus offering some protection.

The round Frankish tower (centre) and the Ottoman bastion (left) flanking the main fortress gate at Argos in southern Greece. (Archive of the American School of Archaeology, Athens).

If an enemy did manage to besiege such difficult locations, they usually faced a series of defended baillies, which made use of the natural topography of the site. Where the terrain did not lend itself to such designs, more regularly planned castles were constructed. The early 13th-century castle at Paphos fell into this second category, and in 1391 King James I of Cyprus built another rectangular castle with corner towers and a surrounding moat at Sivouri, while a similar castle was constructed at La Cava near Nicosia. This style was practically unknown in Greece where castles on hilltops, high or low, almost all relied on one or more enclosed baillies whose curtain walls followed the contours of the rocks, with a few towers being added. In many cases the core of this system consisted of a large donjon, as at Mistra. At Pendeskupi near Corinth the donjon was very simple, while at Clairmont it was polygonal with a small, open courtyard inside. In all cases such fortifications contained water cisterns, some of which were substantial.

By the 15th century Crusader and Italian colonial fortifications faced an increasing threat from gunpowder artillery. One of the most interesting early examples of how they responded is the Hospitaller mainland castle at Bodrum. Located on a narrow isthmus, it consists of a large glacis and a deep ditch excavated down to sea level. Between the glacis and the gate were casemates covered with stone and containing guns that could sweep the area between the glacis and gate. The northern side was protected by two towers joined by a curtain wall and a narrow ditch, while to the west, facing the port, was a broad boulevard.

Tour of the castles

Cyprus

Kyrenia is amongst the best-surviving Crusader coastal fortifications in Cyprus. The late 12th- and early 13th-century castrum next to the harbour was massively strengthened by the Venetians in the 16th century, but the Crusader outer wall still encloses a barrel-vaulted interior with basement galleries. The original medieval plan consisted of a large, square court surrounded by structures built against the curtain walls. At each corner were large, square towers, the north-eastern one being diagonal to the others. There was a postern on the north side, while the main entrance lay across a moat on the west side, defended by a barbican and a drawbridge. The upper of the two storeys above the gate contained a chapel, plus a vestry with an elegant arch over its door.

OPPOSITE PAGE The north-eastern corner of the Genoese castle at Molivos (Methymna) on the island of Lesbos. (Author's photograph)

BELOW The fortifications of the Kingdom of Cyprus (frontiers c. 1328).

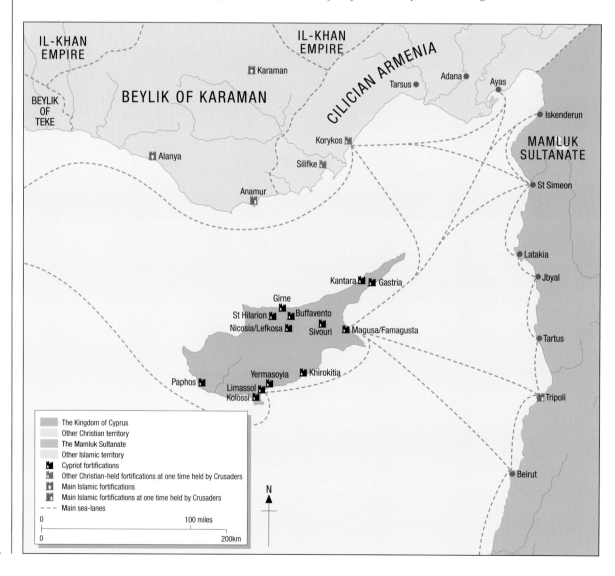

IL-KHAN EMPIRE

IL-KHAN EMPIRE

CILICIAN ARMENIA

BEYLIK OF KARAMAN

BEYLIK OF TEKE

Karaman

Tarsus

Adana

Ayas

Iskenderun

MAMLUK SULTANATE

Korykos

Silifke

Alanya

Anamur

St Simeon

Latakia

Jbyal

Kantara Gastria

Girne

St Hilarion Buffavento

Nicosia/Lefkosa

Sivouri

Magusa/Famagusta

Tartus

Paphos

Yermasoyia Khirokitia

Limassol

Kolossi

Tripoli

Beirut

The Kingdom of Cyprus
Other Christian territory
The Mamluk Sultanate
Other Islamic territory
Cypriot fortifications
Other Christian-held fortifications at one time held by Crusaders
Main Islamic fortifications
Main Islamic fortifications at one time held by Crusaders
Main sea-lanes

N

0   100 miles
0   200km

23

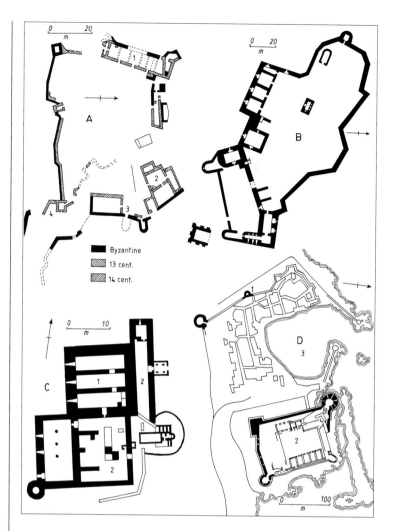

There may originally have been a second, outer barbican or outwork beyond the bridge against the curtain wall. A little church still survives on a small space forming a continuation of the platform on which the castle is built, overlooking the harbour.

According to Fedden, a royal palace overlooked the entrance to Kyrenia castle and the harbour:

This harbour and the bourg behind it were ringed with their own walls, of which several towers survive. Venetian fortification has obscured much of the earlier work. The Venetians entirely rebuilt the outer west wall and, to protect the west and south of the castle, built three ponderous tower-bastions and filled with earth the space between the inner and the outer walls ... On the north and east, where the sea provided its own security and additional fortification seemed superfluous, much Latin work fortunately survives. The fine ashlar masonry speaks of Crusader building. The north curtain, with its two fighting galleries below the parapet whose merlons are pierced for fire, and the elegant horseshoe-shaped tower at the north-east, still indicate the formidable character of the Lusignan fortress.[3]

Cypriot fortifications:

A The upper citadel of St Hilarion Castle showing Byzantine, plus 13th- and 14th-century Crusader structures: 1 – great hall; 2 – kitchen; 3 – gateway; 4 – redoubt (after Enlart).

B Kantara castle (after Enlart).

C The Hospitaller castle at Kolossi: 1 – donjon; 2 – outbuildings (after Megaw).

D The fortified town and castle at Kyrenia: 1 – remains of the city wall; 2 – citadel; 3 – harbour (after Enlart).

St Hilarion is a typically dramatic example of a Crusader mountain-top castle in Cyprus. It had already been fortified by the regent Jean d'Ibelin around 1228, perhaps as a retreat for the heir apparent and his sisters who felt threatened by Emperor Frederick II. Here the Crusaders improved upon the three separate stages or levels of existing Byzantine fortification. The large outermost bailey lay to the south. Its rather feeble Byzantine rubble wall and circular towers remained largely unchanged, though the gate did have a machicolation. A steep corridor climbed from this outer bailey to the second level. Here it is interesting to note that, at an altitude of around 700m, the medieval builders used pitched roofs to resist heavy winter snowfalls rather than the flat roofs characteristic of most other Crusader architecture in the eastern Mediterranean. The third level of fortification was to the west of the second level and can only be reached by another steep climb. To the north, south, and west of the castle breathtaking cliffs and very steep slopes remove the threat of serious assault. Lying between the two rocky summits is a small area of which the eastern or entrance side is protected by fortification. Immediately to the west are buildings whose finely carved doors and windows show that this was the *cour d'honneur* of what was, in effect, both a palace and a castle.[4]

[3] Fedden, R. *Crusader Castles: A Brief Study in the Military Architecture of the Crusades* (London, 1950), 113.
[4] Ibid, 115-7.

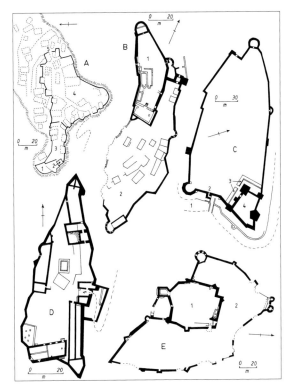

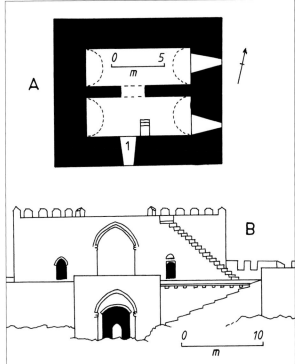

Mainland Greece

Mistra, to the west of the town of Sparti in the Peloponnese, is better known for its late Byzantine wall paintings and churches than for the Crusader castle that dominates the site. The latter was constructed for William de Villehardouin in 1249 and consists of a donjon and inner enceinte on the topmost ridge, with a lower enceinte beneath. The 13th-century Crusader castle was subsequently repaired by the Byzantine Greeks or the Ottoman Turks. Its main entrance is protected by a large, rectangular tower, and there are semi-circular towers in the circuit walls. The inner enceinte is surrounded by a second wall with a gate into the outer bailey. A small chapel embedded in the southern battlements apparently existed before the castle was built. A substantial round tower on the north-eastern side is near a large underground water cistern, and there was another cistern beneath a massive rectangular building at the eastern end of the upper citadel, which in turn served as the commanders' residence. On the highest part of the western edge of the summit is another semi-circular tower facing a dangerous tribal area in the mountains beyond.

Clairmont (Chlemutzi) is by far the finest fortified structure dating from the Crusader period on the Greek mainland. From here Geoffrey III de Villehardouin commandeered the church revenues, a role which enabled him to spend much more on the site than elsewhere. It took three years to build (1220–23), defended the town of Clarenza, and overlooked the main harbour – though from a distance. The existing castle of Clairmont consists of a large keep with an inner court on top of the hill, plus an outer bailey on the sides most vulnerable to attack. Accommodation inside the keep appears to have been comfortable and well lit. It was cool in summer, while fireplaces, one above the other on each floor, ensured warmth in winter. Clairmont was, in fact, clearly a centre for courtly life. The outer bailey and its wall were, however, altered during the Ottoman period and have recently been restored. Furthermore, the dating of the keep itself remains a matter of debate. Its plan is very different from other medieval castles in Greece. The method of forming a courtyard by great

LEFT Large Greek mainland fortifications:

A Vardounia castle: 1 – keep; 2 – tower; 3 – inner court; 4 – outer court; 5 – lower gate (after Burridge).

B The castle of Mistra: 1 – citadel; 2 – lower ward (after Bon).

C The citadel of Patras: 1 – outer moat; 2 – main gate; 3 – inner moat; 4 – keep (after Bon).

D The castle of Karytaina (after Bon).

E The citadel of Argos: 1 – keep; 2 – outer ward (after Bon).

RIGHT Small Greek mainland fortifications:

A The Crusader tower at Thebes: 1 – modern entrance, not existing in the medieval period (after Bon).

B The interior of the Southern Sea Gate at Methoni, 15th-century Venetian (after Andrews).

Destruction of the Castle of Forty Columns at Paphos by an earthquake, 1222

Destruction of the Castle of Forty Columns at Paphos by an earthquake, 1222

The ruined castle that overlooks the bay and town of Paphos in Cyprus was badly damaged by an earthquake even before its construction was finished. How much work remained to be done is unclear, and much of the fallen masonry was subsequently taken as building material for the town of Paphos itself. Clearly the castle was no longer considered important enough for work to be restarted, presumably because the conquest of the Byzantine capital of Constantinople (Istanbul) by the Fourth Crusade removed the threat from Byzantium. In this reconstruction the main walls and towers are virtually complete, showing the castle to have been of a classic concentric design. Although some historians suggest that the basic design of at least the central part of this castle was Byzantine, dating from as early as the 7th or 8th centuries, any existing Byzantine structures would be embedded within or beneath the inner keep. This keep consisted of four massive towers around a small inner courtyard, plus a semi-circular entrance tower projecting a considerable distance from one side. The outer walls and towers were separate from the inner complex, making Paphos castle genuinely concentric. The corner towers of the outer defences were relatively small, including three round and one polygonal design. There were also triangular or prow-shaped towers in the middle of two sides of the outer wall, with a small rectangular tower in the middle of the third. Slightly offset from the centre of the fourth side (on the left in our reconstruction) was a massive rectangular entrance tower. Behind this was an entrance bridge across the dry moat, abutting the outer wall at a point where the wall itself was slightly angled.

LEFT The medieval castle (right) dominates the Bay of Parga on the Ionian coast of northern Greece. Disputed between the Latin rulers of the offshore islands and the local Orthodox Christians rulers of the mainland, it was ceded to Venice in 1401. (Bob Rankin)

surrounding halls, the monumental character of this court, the double external staircases to the principal rooms of the main floor, the wooden floors of these rooms, and the numerous and well-constructed fireplaces, all seem more characteristic of the 15th century. Ramsay Traquair also noted Clairmont's similarity with the 15th-century Italian castle of Bracciano, and the Ottoman Turkish Anadolu Hisar castle on the Bosphoros.

The castle of Patras was a very strong fortress, which, in 1429, resisted a year-long siege by the Byzantine ruler Constantine – even after he had captured the town. It consists of a keep with a central citadel and a large courtyard. The walls clearly date from at least two separate periods and the lower parts of the keep, particularly on the northern side of the court, incorporate many classical fragments, whereas the upper parts of the structure comprise rubble. On the east wall of the keep are the remains of stone corbels, which originally supported the hoardings of the Crusader castle. According to Traquair, writing just over a hundred years ago before the more recent changes to this site:

The entrance is on the south side by a fine vaulted gatehouse, the sheeted iron doors are still in use, and above the arch is a little huchette on two

The keep or donjon of Chlemutzi (Clairmont) castle in southern Greece. (Ian Meigh)

The enceinte of Chlemutzi (Clairmont) castle, showing the main gate. This was originally set inside a deep recess in the outer defences, the size of which is indicated by a vertical 'crease' in the wall, just to the right of the existing entrance. (Ian Meigh)

brackets. The western end of the court, and particularly the south-western tower, are fine example of Italian fortification; the tower is octagonal ... The defence is in two stories, a battlemented rampart above, with under it, a range of chambers and loopholes. The plan is typically medieval and is probably very little changed from the castle so ruthlessly constructed by Aleman, to whom we may attribute the greater part of the keep walls and the northern wall of the court. To Italian influence are due the notched battlements, and at some time in the fifteenth century an extensive reconstruction must have taken place which included the upper parts of the keep walls, the gatehouse and the southern and western walls of the court, with their octagonal towers ... The later Turkish repairs are easily distinguishable by their plastered surface. Patras is in some ways the most interesting of Greek castles; it is still in fairly good preservation and has never been completely rebuilt, unlike so many of the famous Frankish castles whose sites are now marked only by crumbling Turkish walls.[5]

Platamon (Pandeleimon) is the best-preserved Crusader castle in north-central Greece. It is on a naturally defensible site overlooking a strategic pass. King Boniface of Thessaloniki gave the site to a northern Italian knight named Orlando Pischia, and ordered him to build a castle. The resulting fortress has three enclosures, the outermost being particularly large, with its main entrance

[5] Traquair, R. 'Laconia. I – Medieval Fortresses', *The Annual of the British School at Athens*, 12 (1905–6), 280–1.

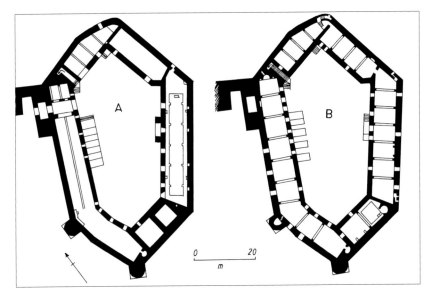

LEFT The donjon of the castle of Chlemutzi (Clairmont).
A Ground floor (after Bon).
B First floor (after Bon).

on the south-eastern side where there was another ruined outer wall or perhaps a barbican. Today the walls are still from 7.5–9.5m high, 1.2–2m thick, with towers of varying size and design, spaced at irregular intervals where the wall changes direction. Between the inner and outer gates of the main entrance there was once a large tower. The second wall is 6–7m high with, in the north-east corner, an unusual tower that is square outside and round inside, with a Byzantine-style tiled dome on top. Another wall 1m thick and 5.25m high surrounds a large octagonal tower, which served as the central keep. It is 16m high with walls 2m thick, having its entrance 3.45m above the ground and reached by a wooden staircase. This tower has semi-circular windows, one having two openings with a small central column decorated with a cross, and it may date from after the Crusader period when the castle of Platamon was repaired for the Byzantine Despotate of Arta.

The Aegean

The citadel of Chios, on the eponymous island, is a good example of Genoese colonial fortification. Here the Zaccaria family from Genoa built a new fortress under Byzantine suzerainty around 1328, on the site of an existing *kastron*.

FOLLOWING PAGES

The castle of Clairmont (Chlemutzi)

The dating of the castle of Clairmont remains a matter of debate. Most historians believe that it was built by the prince of Achaea in the 13th century, but some suggest that the prince's castle is marked by unexcavated ruins closer to the shore. They also maintain that the existing castle dates from as late as the 15th century. The entrance through the outer wall or enceinte was modified and strengthened at some time after the original construction, either by the last Crusader lords, the Byzantines, or perhaps the first Ottoman Turkish occupiers. The hilltop castle had a keep on the summit, overlooking the steepest side of the hill. A polygonal enceinte or outer wall extends around the other, more gently sloping side of the hill. The masonry of the keep, though not the enceinte, is of a higher standard than is

seen in other Crusader castles in Greece. The merlons of the crenellations on the enceinte are alternately pierced – but not for archery. In addition to the main gate through the enceinte there were at least two small postern gates, one of them close to the main entrance to the keep from the inner ward. There were also steps from the ward to the top of the enceinte at this point. Within the ward were numerous buildings, some of them clearly from the Ottoman period, though most of the structures attached to the inside of the outer fortified wall probably dated from the earlier centuries. The unroofed enclosures in the ward are more difficult to date but were presumably pens for horses or food animals. The size and number of the windows in the outer wall, and the fact that this enceinte had only one, small, half-round tower suggests that its defensive potential was limited. Resistance to a determined attack had to rely on the keep.

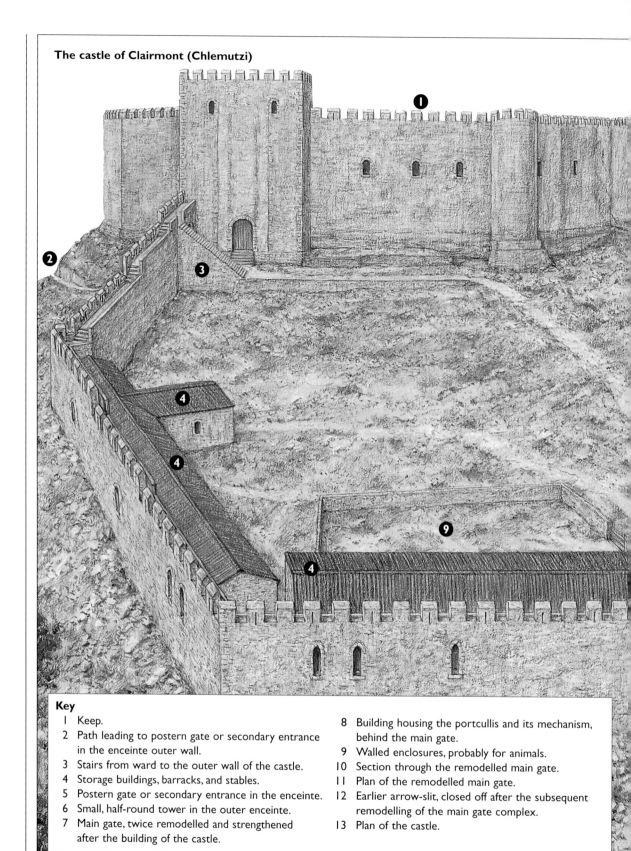

The castle of Clairmont (Chlemutzi)

Key

1 Keep.
2 Path leading to postern gate or secondary entrance in the enceinte outer wall.
3 Stairs from ward to the outer wall of the castle.
4 Storage buildings, barracks, and stables.
5 Postern gate or secondary entrance in the enceinte.
6 Small, half-round tower in the outer enceinte.
7 Main gate, twice remodelled and strengthened after the building of the castle.
8 Building housing the portcullis and its mechanism, behind the main gate.
9 Walled enclosures, probably for animals.
10 Section through the remodelled main gate.
11 Plan of the remodelled main gate.
12 Earlier arrow-slit, closed off after the subsequent remodelling of the main gate complex.
13 Plan of the castle.

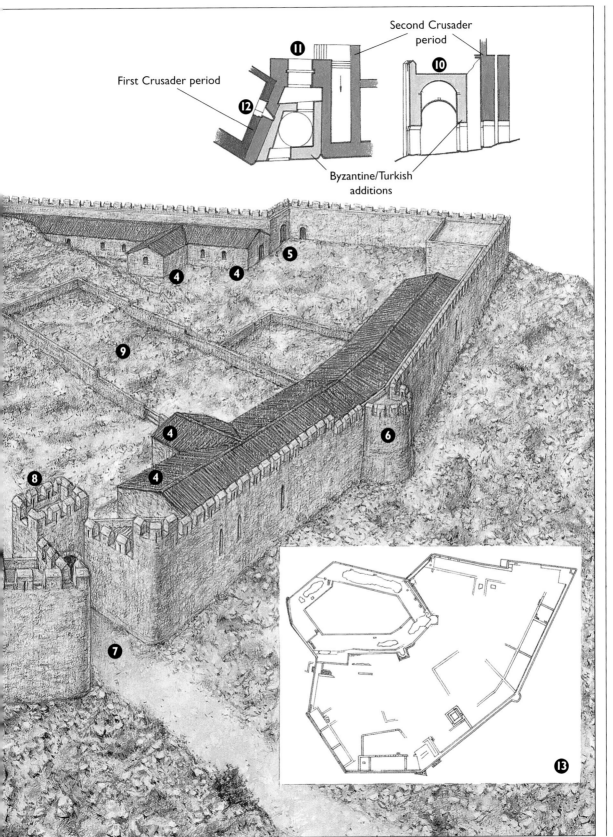

First Crusader period

Second Crusader period

Byzantine/Turkish additions

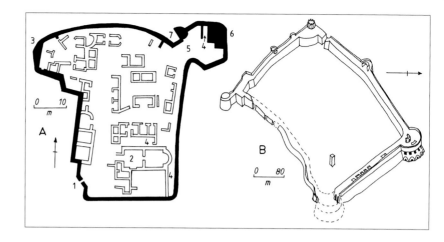

Greek island fortifications:
A   The fortified village of Megalo
    Horio on the island of Tilos:
    1 – entrance; 2 – church;
    3 – possible artillery platform;
    4 – water storage areas;
    5 – inner bailley; 6 – tower;
    7 – possible postern gate
    (after Short).
B   Simplified representation of the
    Genoese citadel or *castrum* of
    Chios, showing the damaged
    south-eastern wall and the
    destroyed eastern tower
    (after Fedden).

Black Sea fortifications:
A   The Genoese and Byzantine
    fortifications of Amasra:
    1 – fortifications on the island
    of Boz Tepe; 2 – fortified bridge;
    3 – main land walls; 4 – citadel;
    5 – western outer gate;
    6 – eastern gate; 7 – sea
    (after Crow).
B   The medieval fortification of
    Kaffa, according to an Ottoman
    map of 1784: 1 – gates in the
    land walls of the city; 2 – Tower
    of Constantine; 3 – citadel;
    4 – *castrum*; 5 – main port.
C   The fortress of
    Bilhorod-Dnistrovsky
    (Moncastro): 1 – Genoese castle;
    2 –15th-century inner ward;
    3 – large outbuilding;
    4 – 15th-century outer ward;
    5 – moat (after Ionescu).

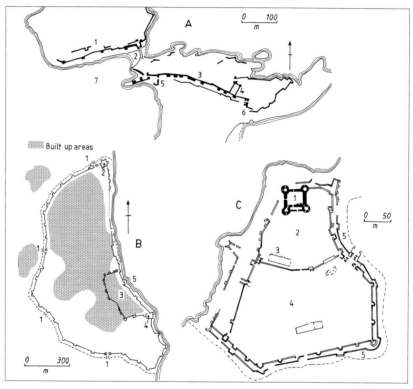

This was taken by another Genoese, Simone Vignoso, in 1346, after which the Genoese *Mahone*, or local colonial authorities, modified its defences still further. The result was a large, five-sided, fortified enclosure of which three sides faced the Greek town, the fourth dominated the port, and the fifth overlooked the coast. The walls were improved or repaired in the second half of the 15th century and in its final form the fortress had nine towers equally spaced along all the walls except that facing the sea. Surviving documents also mention two gates leading to the market area of the town, and one facing the port. The fact that the wall facing the port was also the weakest indicates that the Genoese expected trouble from the land and the open sea, but did not expect to lose control of their harbour.[6]

---

[6] For a discussion of the Hospitaller fortifications of Rhodes and Bodrum, see also Osprey Warrior 41: *Knight Hospitaller (2): 1306–1565*.

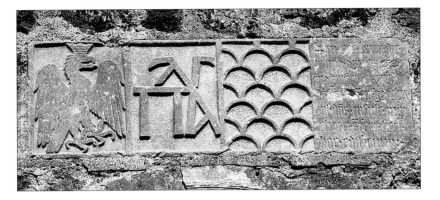

The combined coats-of-arms of Francesco I Gattelusi, the Genoese ruler of the island of Lesbos (1355–85), and his wife, a Byzantine princess, carved above the entrance of the Kastro of Myteleni. (Author's photograph)

The Black Sea

Amasra was not the most important fortified Italian commercial outpost in the Black Sea but it is an interesting example of how a western European maritime power used existing Byzantine fortifications, only modifying them where it was really necessary to do so. Here the small island of Boz Tepe was so close to the shore, being separated by shallow water and a beach, that it could be linked to the mainland by a fortified bridge. Behind this was a powerful wall and towers to protect the southern side of the island. On the mainland immediately opposite was a citadel now called the İç Kale. In addition the walls and towers of the southern or inland-facing fortifications protected the coastal hill on which the town itself sat. Most of the fortifications are Byzantine, dating from before the 14th-century Genoese occupation, and include emplacements for both traction-powered and perhaps also torsion-powered pre-gunpowder artillery. The Genoese then converted some of the arrow-slits to make them into gun-ports for early cannon. Since the main threat to Amasra came from inland, the strongest fortifications were located here, comprising at least two lines of walls in the most vulnerable sections. The Genoese colonial authorities also increased the height of some walls and towers. The main inner wall is still well preserved, with projecting rectangular towers of various sizes and shapes, between 6 and 9m wide and projecting 4–6m. One much longer tower near the centre of the wall is nearly 23m across but only projects about 2m. Many of these towers have a solid core. Some alterations to the gates are thought to be Genoese, including the addition of machicolations on the secondary gate. On the İç Kale the Genoese inserted a new wall to create a sort of keep on the west side. This was entered at first-floor level above a blocked Byzantine door. Here other strengthening included projecting corbels, huchettes, and machicolations in the western European tradition of military architecture, plus further gun-ports. Other than these modifications, the most visible relics of the Italian occupation are a number of carved stone heraldic panels. Those over the entrances to the İç Kale display the arms of the Republic of Genoa flanked by those of the powerful Poggio and Malaspina families.

The fortifications of Kaffa on the Crimean peninsula of what is now Ukraine were far more extensive. Little remains today, but most seem to be 14th-century Genoese work built upon the foundations or along the lines of earlier Byzantine defences. The outer wall was almost 5.5km long, forming an arc around the town, outside an inner wall, and joining up with the sea wall. According to the Ottoman Turkish traveller Evliya Celebi, writing in the 17th century, this wall had 117 bastions, with an exterior dry ditch 13.5m deep and 33.5m across. There was no ditch along the coast. Instead the sea gates opened directly onto the beach to make the loading and unloading of goods easier. The Ottomans called the third line of defence at Kaffa the 'land fortress'. Outside the main, strongly defended city the suburbs were protected only by a simple embankment during the later Genoese period. These, however, have all but disappeared.

The Galata Tower, built by the Genoese as the key point in their defence of Pera (modern Galata) in Istanbul. (Author's photograph)

The living sites

The Crusader conquest of central and southern Greece was carried by a remarkably small number of knights and mounted sergeants, with infantry rarely mentioned. The states that emerged were even shorter on loyal military manpower than the Crusader States of the Middle East. After the fall of the ephemeral Crusader Kingdom of Thessalonika to the Byzantine Despotate of Epirus, all that remained was the increasingly feeble Latin 'empire' of Constantinople, which fell in 1261, and the remarkably enduring Principality of Achaea, which also included the Duchy of Athens.

In Greece, fertile land was scarce and few baronies could be created. They ranged in size from four to eight fiefs, though the number of fiefs subsequently increased; by 1377 a list mentioned 51 castles, some of them very small. The exposed nature of these Crusader states meant that feudal military obligations of four months, plus four more on castle guard, were firmly enforced during the 13th century. By the mid 14th century, however, the military enthusiasm of the Latin or western European aristocracy had declined, and personal military service was gradually replaced by a tax called the *adoha*. There were also differences between various Crusader-ruled regions – for example, a feudal structure never took root in central Greece. In contrast, the conquerors of the south managed to establish a society based upon a French model.

Subsequent Italian and Spanish occupiers introduced other, later variations of the feudal model. At the same time the ex-Byzantine elites, not all of them Greek, increased in influence because they were more numerous than the westerners, and their military allegiance had to be encouraged. Nevertheless, there is no evidence that these indigenous groups had specific associations with local fortifications – even with the small rural towers.

In Cyprus the ownership of fortifications remained a royal prerogative, except for a few castles built by the Military Orders. Instead, the Latin aristocracy largely lived in towns, and their rural manors were rarely fortified. There were similarly few castles in Crusader-ruled central Greece, despite this being an exposed and vulnerable frontier area. Instead it seems to have been dominated by an anarchic elite of knights and sergeants who could only afford to build modest towers.

Castles were more abundant in southern Greece, where their primary function was apparently to store and display wealth. At first the hugely outnumbered Crusaders mostly lived in isolated mountain-top castles and fortified rural mansions, confident in their military superiority, though many also had town houses. Most of the major citadels were controlled by the ruler rather than the barons, the Castle of Sathines on the Acropolis of Athens and the Kadmeia fortress in Thebes being under military governors appointed by the prince. After the Angevin rulers of southern Italy took over Achaea in 1278, the area was governed by officials, who were in charge of the main castles and garrisons.

Once the Crusader aristocracy started paying the *adoha* tax rather than offering personal military service, castle garrisons increasingly consisted of mercenaries. Their pay varied according to circumstances, but an ordnance of Nicolas de Joinville (1323–25) was seemingly intended to fix the pay for men-at-arms at 800 *hyperperes* per year if the soldier came from overseas, and 600 if he was local. Squires would be paid 400 and 300 respectively. Many 'local' troops were now Greek in culture and military tradition, though some converted to Catholic Christianity to be accepted by the ruling elite. The latter were now increasingly Italian in origin and outlook, being much less feudally minded than the previous French aristocracy. Large military contingents were sent from Italy after the Angevin takeover, along with specialists like doctors and military engineers, though some garrisons were still not paid for a long time. It is interesting to note that amongst the troops the Angevin ruler sent to his garrisons in Albania in the 1270s were hundreds of Muslim 'Saracens from Lucera', mostly archers and crossbowmen. But as a shortage of troops became more serious, the Angevins increasingly recruited Greeks and Albanians – a pool of manpower that was also vital to the Byzantine rulers of this region.

Little is known about the arsenals that clearly existed in several fortresses. Archaeologists uncovered a large store of crossbow boltheads in the castle at Paphos, along with about 1,500 stone mangonel balls, seemingly stored on a terrace that collapsed during the earthquake. Documentary sources mention crossbows being manufactured in an arsenal on Corfu under Angevin rule, while the Angevins certainly established an armoury in the castle of Clarenza in 1281, to maintain weaponry shipped from Italy.

While the castle at Thebes was usually the main residence of the duke of Athens, the entrance complex of the Acropolis of Athens was eventually converted into a ducal palace. Known as the Mnesikles, it was described as a fine *palazzo* by the later Italian dukes. How strongly it was fortified is much less clear. In complete contrast were the isolated towers that dotted the Duchy of Athens. There were many others on the Venetian-ruled island of Euboea and in the Peloponnese. Such towers may have expressed the power and status of the non-noble but militarily significant sergeant level of Crusader society. Most were small and simple, but some resembled small castles with curtain walls. The little documentary evidence that survives includes a reference to the tower at Krestena being repaired in 1354 when it was said to have had a gilded roof, a drawbridge, and a private residential apartment.

In addition to a few fortified towns and cities, the Crusader States also included some fortified monasteries, including Dafni, which was inhabited by Cistercian monks during the Crusader period. They demolished the upper floor of what had been a library or abbot's residence at the western end of the church, and added defensive battlements. The Ottoman Sultan returned the monastery to Greek Orthodox monks in 1458, and it is unclear whether the fortified curtain wall dates from this or from the Crusader occupation.

Where Crusader fortresses were used as residences, they could be remarkably comfortable. In Cyprus the mountain-top castle of Kyrenia may have been used as a summer retreat from the sultry lowlands. In Greece some early 13th-century castles reflected the home life of the knightly elite of France of Burgundy from which most of the conquerors came. Clermont, which dated from rather later, contained an unusual number of fireplaces, latrines, and the water cisterns, which made life more comfortable.

Residential castles certainly helped the new military rulers retain their cultural and physical separation from the Greek Orthodox majority. In Cyprus this separation remained almost complete until the second half of the 14th century, the dominant Latins using costume, military ceremonial, and military architecture to proclaim their distinctiveness. In the late 13th-century Greece, the castle at Thebes was described as being highly decorated and 'big enough for an emperor and his court'. French remained the language of the knightly class in Cyprus and Greece until partially replaced by Italian in the 14th century. The culture and society of the new rulers were, according to contemporary sources, extremely refined. Raymond Muntaner wrote that 'the most noble French knights were the knights of the Morea [Peloponnese] who spoke as good French as that of Paris'. Early 13th-century literature from Cyprus was in the same tradition as that of both France and the Crusader States of the Holy Land, while literary works from later 13th-century Crusader Greece were similar to those of French-ruled southern Italy. In both areas there was a strong interest in the history of the Crusades as well as Arthurian legends and ancient Greek myths, particularly those concerning battles against the Amazons. On the other

Decorating the Great Hall of Kadmeia castle at Thebes, late 13th century

The Kadmeia fortress or castle at Thebes was built between 1258 and 1280 for Nicholas II de St Omer. Most of this castle has been destroyed, including the famous hall, which was originally decorated with wall paintings illustrating the conquest of Syria by the First Crusade. These may have been made, or at least designed, by artists from the Crusader Principality of Antioch in northern Syria, brought to Thebes by Nicholas' wife, Mary of Antioch. This reconstruction is based upon written evidence, upon comparable but surviving Crusader architecture from the same period, and upon late 13th-century manuscript illustrations of various sieges during the First Crusade. The traditional method of making wall paintings shown in our reconstruction is illustrated in many medieval manuscripts and is still practised in various parts of the Balkans and Greece. A senior artist paints over the initial sketches while his assistants mix plaster in a wooden vat and add the fibrous material that strengthens the layer of plaster.

RIGHT The Byzantine monastery at Dafni was surrounded by fortified walls during the Crusader occupation. (Author's photograph)

hand, this cultural brilliance faded in the 14th century in Crusader Greece, which became little more than a collection of outposts dominated by powers from Italy and Spain.

Wall paintings similarly helped the Crusaders keep in touch with their western European cultural roots. The 'Destruction of Troy' decorated the Catholic archbishop's palace at Patras, while the 'Conquest of Syria' by the First Crusade was painted on some walls in the Kadmeia castle in Thebes; the artists may actually have been brought from northern Syria by Mary of Antioch, wife of Nicholas II of St Omer.

Some of the earliest wall painting from Crusader-ruled Cyprus has interesting similarities with the art of the ex-Byzantine provinces of what is now Turkey, rather than that of the Byzantine capital. Very little art survives from Crusader Greece, and what does is mostly primitive, a few churches being decorated with geometric or simplified scroll patterns. Crudely carved heraldic animals within circles and heraldic shields were popular and there are also decorative elements drawn from Islamic art, though it is unclear whether these came from Crusader Syria, the residual Muslim communities of southern Italy, or reflected the influence of Muslim mercenary soldiers hired by some Crusader lords from the mid 13th century onwards.

One might have expected the new rulers to make use of the ancient Greek statues and relief carvings, and the well-cut architectural fragments scattered across the country. However, the Crusader occupiers of Corinth did not apparently reuse such artefacts in a visible way; instead, they used ancient statues as building material. Only in the 15th century did attitudes begin to change, but even at this later date, most marble carvings and statues were rendered down as lime for mortar or concrete. Only a few scholars and travellers, influenced by new Humanist ideas, tried to preserve relics of Classical civilization.

Decorating the Great Hall of Kadmeia castle at Thebes, late 13th century

There was a Byzantine influence on the home life of the Crusader aristocracy in both Greece and Cyprus, just as there was an Islamic influence in the Crusader States of the Middle East. The one sphere in which this influence was rejected was, of course, religion since it was the newcomers' Catholic identity that set them apart. At the same time there was a localized Crusader influence on the ruling classes of neighbouring Byzantine states, the cultural and political situation being especially complex in Epirus in what is now north-western Greece and southern Albania. This was feudalized under later Italianized or Italian despots like Leonardo III Tocco who held three castles on the mainland plus several off-shore islands. As a result, several castles became the hereditary property of Greek, Serb, Albanian, and Italian soldiers in the late 14th and 15th centuries.

Life in the fortified outposts of the Italian maritime empires had different priorities. We also know more about it because detailed records survive in Venice and Genoa. The situation was, however, complicated by the fact that some places changed hands several times. The island of Lemnos was in Crusader hands from 1204 to 1279. Thereafter it was disputed between Venetians, Genoese, and Byzantines until the Byzantines gave authority to the autonomous Genoese Gattilusi family in 1414. From 1462 until 1479 it was disputed by the Venetians and Ottoman Turks. With such a history it is hardly surprising that Lemnos is dotted with castles, watch towers, and fortified monasteries. The castles at Kotsinas and Palaiokastro were then damaged by earthquake in 1470, after which Kotsinas was not rebuilt.

Venice and Genoa governed their colonial outposts in different ways, the Venetian colonial authorities generally following central government orders closely and reflecting the centralized character of the Venetian Republic. Venetian colonies, with the exception of Crete, also often had small populations and initially archaic fortifications, but these were well maintained. For example, the Venetian merchant quarter at Tana (Azov) north of the Black Sea was fortified in the early 14th century, being given a small garrison under a consul and two counsellors, a system similar to that in other outposts under direct Venetian rule.

Most Venetian fortresses in Greece differed from those of the Crusaders, mostly being on the coasts and usually guarding harbours.[7] They were intended to resist attack from land or sea, and sometimes an entire bay was encircled by walls that extended into moles, virtually enclosing the harbour. At Kyrenia, Herakleion, and Chanea the Venetians built a wall facing the sea and ramparts facing the land. At Naupaktos two defensive walls descended from a cliff-edged hill straight to the shore then curved out into the water to form a tiny harbour. In several other places the Venetians occupied a peninsula and, using any fortifications that existed, walled it from end to end and constructed moles to shelter ships. Later they cut off some peninsulas with moats, backed by massive fortifications.

Pay for garrisons depended on rank, the importance of the fortress, and the current military situation. Initially, mercenaries in Venetian Greece received two or three ducats a month, the same as an oarsman in a galley, though this later rose to three to four ducats. The chatelain of a small town like Argos might be paid five ducats, whereas the commanders of important garrisons like Korone and Methoni received sixteen and a half ducats a month in 1341. Seventeen years later the Venetian Senate authorized the chatelain of Methoni to hire 300 mercenaries. Methoni is an interesting example of how Venetian colonists were settled, and their subsequent way of life. In 1293 the Senate ordered the walls of Methoni and Korone to be rebuilt and the towns to be populated by 24 families sent from Venice. Inside the *burgus*, or fortified town, of Methoni were commercial warehouses. There were market places inside the *burgus* and the *castrum*, supplying food and drink for passing pilgrims, travellers, and sailors, though there was a separate bakery for the navy. Lodgings were reserved

---

[7] See also Osprey Men-at-Arms 210: *The Venetian Empire 1200–1670*.

The walls of the *kastro* or castle of Myteleni enclose a very large area. In castles of comparable extent, such land was sometimes used to grow crops – a characteristic of several fortifications built by western European rulers in later medieval Greece. (Author's photograph)

for Jewish travellers, and a hospital dedicated to St Iohannes looked after sick pilgrims and merchants.

Although Methoni was of only secondary importance, considerable efforts were made to keep its harbour operational. However, the mole was often damaged by storms, and this impressive structure could not entirely protect ships from severe weather. One 15th-century map called the Parma Magliabecchi recommended that only small craft anchor inside the mole, and in 1477 a Venetian admiral and the castellan of Methoni jointly reported that, due to the previous winter's storms, the port was so silted up that even shallow-draught war-galleys could not enter. Orders of 1395 that a new gate be built linking the *castrum* to the port caused further difficulties; several houses were demolished and replaced by lodgings for the soldiers guarding the new gate, plus a *platea* (open space) was created, probably with a customs house and public warehouses.

The troops garrisoning the fortresses of the four military districts of Venetian Crete usually numbered about 30 men each. Their primary role was to combat pirates and bandits while the inhabitants of the main colonial towns defended their own walls. In 1394 the *baillo* in Durazzo (now Dürres in Albania) also had 30 'new' crossbowmen in the two castles under his control.

As the threat from Ottoman raiders increased in the 15th century, small local defences were built to protect Greek villages close to the main Venetian fortresses in the southern Peloponnese. By late summer 1410 the Senate recorded that several small forts on the Korone peninsula had towers, walls, and *burghi*, in addition to work done on the existing *burghi* and *isola* (or fortified island) of Korone itself. These enabled local peasants to store their corn, wine, and oil in safety before all such stores were brought into Korone during November.

The account of a pilgrimage to the Holy Land supposedly made by Arnold von Harff in 1496–99 is sometimes dismissed as a fable, but its German author clearly drew upon travellers' observations even if he never went on pilgrimage himself. In his description of Methoni he stated:

> This town of Modon is very strong. It is subject to the Venetians, and the land belonging to it is called Morea, which lies near to Turkey (the territory of the Turkish Ottoman Sultan) ... I found there a German master-gunner called Peter Bombadere, who gave me good company and friendship. He showed me the strength of the town and the artillery, and it is in truth a small town but strong. On the land side it has three suburbs with three walls and three ditches hewn out of the natural rock, on which they are building daily. He took me round the innermost wall which was very thick and built of rough stones; in addition there is a rampart against the wall on which stand many fine cannon, great carthouns [meaning unknown] and slings.'[8]

[8] von Harff, Arnold (tr. M. Letts) *The Pilgrimage of Arnold von Harff, Knight* (London, 1946), 80–1.

Part of a late 14th- or 15th-century wall painting showing St George slaying the dragon, in the English Chapel of St George, Rhodes (ex-Baron de Belabre).

At Karaman in Turkey, the local museum has a very early bronze cannon, which was probably one of those supplied by Venice to their ally, the Turkish Aq Qoyunlu, ruler of eastern Turkey, around 1470. A document in the Venice State Archives notes:

> There are in our Arsenal three moulds for bombards made by Bartolomeo da Cremona, which throw 100 lb. stones, and to cast them are needed 18 milliara [1,000 lb.] of copper and 240 lb. of tin. And, as everybody knows, it is necessary to provide because of our obligations with his highness Ussani Cassani ... [The rest of this document concerns the order to cast 50 small guns][9]

Genoese colonial outposts were governed in a different way, reflecting the fragmented nature of authority in the Republic of Genoa. They tended to be largely autonomous, with local governors or almost independent feudal lords having their own small garrisons. These troops maintained internal security while Genoese fleets kept trade flowing. The *Mahone* or local Genoese authorities preferred a minimal garrison to avoid alienating the local inhabitants, most of whom were Orthodox Christian Greeks, Armenians, and others. In dealings with their powerful neighbours, these tiny outposts normally relied on money and

---

[9] Archivio di Stato di Venezia – Senato – Deliberazioni Terra, Reg., 191v – December 21, 1472. I am grateful to Prof. Marco Morin for supplying this previously unpublished information.

diplomacy to maintain good relations. While the soldiers in their garrisons rarely remained in one place for long, those who lived in such Genoese enclaves often had houses in the unfortified suburbs, where there were also mills, orchards, and vineyards.

By the late 14th century, Genoa had about 11 castles to defend its scattered possessions, but the large island of Chios remained the only colony with a sizeable population of Geneose origin. Here the Gattilusio family, which also ruled Lesbos and some smaller enclaves, relied on the goodwill of the more numerous indigenous population, real Gattilusio power being confined to the fortress overlooking the main town. Genoese enclaves on the northern coast of Turkey often had tense relations with the Byzantine emperor of Trebizond (Trabzon), who usually favoured Venice. They were also exposed to attack by Turkish rulers of the interior.

The Genoese presence at Kaffa in the Crimea dated from the 1270s, when the Mongol Khan gave the Genoese and Venetians joint permission to establish a settlement. The Venetians eventually lost their foothold after the Byzantines regained Constantinople and gave privileges to the Genoese. Kaffa now grew into a prosperous city, and by the start of the 15th century the captured Crusader squire, Iohan Schiltberger, claimed it had 6,000 houses within its fortified wall, with 11,000 outside and a further 4,000 houses in a more distant suburb. The true population of Kaffa in the late 14th century was around 20,000 people, including Greeks, Armenians, and Russians who lived outside the fortified *castrum* and *civitas*. At the start of the 14th century the Caput Gazarie local governor was under the Genoese consul in Pera, but later the governor of Kaffa became responsible for the defence of all the Genoese outposts around the Black Sea in addition to the gate-guards, military equipment, naval construction facilities, and galleys based in Kaffa.

The extraordinarily detailed Genoese colonial records emphasize the importance of fully trained crossbowmen – a man capable of repairing as well as using crossbows being even more valued – and such skills were a useful qualification for anyone wanting to find work in Kaffa. Crossbowmen also indulged in local trading, sometimes pledging their weapons and ammunition as collateral in commercial agreements. Given the size of Kaffa, and the length of the coastal strip dominated by Genoa, garrisons in the Crimea seem surprisingly small. In 1369 the *podestà*, or senior military officer, had only 25 crossbowmen in Kaffa while in 1386 the population of Kaffa included Greeks building ships, and blacksmiths making arrowheads and bombards, or early cannon. The Genoese *podestà* at Pera had 12 sergeants in 1390 and a year later there were a mere 40 soldiers in the Genoese garrison of Magusa in Cyprus.

On the north-western side of the Black Sea another group of fortified Genoese commercial outposts included Bilhorod-Dnistrovsky, which the Genoese knew as Moncastro, Kiliya, and perhaps a third on the island of Giurgiu further up the River Danube. Early Genoese documents show that Genoese formed a third of the residents of western European origin around 1300, other Italians including Corsicans, Piedmontese, and Lombards. At first there seemed little need for serious fortifications, but after the middle of the 14th century the local Genoese began to feel threatened by the rising power of the Ottoman Turks. At Bilhorod-Dnistrovsky they built a rectangular citadel with four massive round corner towers. This still exists, although it is difficult to differentiate between Genoese construction of the 14th and 15th centuries, and the substantial strengthening done by Moldavian rulers like Alexandru the Good and Steven the Great. At Kiliya a ruined island fortress in the Danube was probably the Genoese castle, while fragmentary fortifications on the left bank were the fortress of Steven the Great. In fact the Genoese lost Kiliya to the Wallachians, from whom Steven the Great took the fortress in 1465, though most of the population remained Italian merchants. Eventually Genoese and Moldavians attempted to cooperate against the looming Ottoman Empire, but failed.

The castles at war

Although many Crusader castles outside the Middle East seem to have had a more symbolic than military value, many were of course used in war. In Cyprus only the coastal fortifications could be described as strong, and there was little threat from the interior as long as the Greek population were cowed into accepting western domination. In contrast, the coasts were exposed to attack from Mamluks, rival Christian powers, and Ottoman Turks.

Things were different in the Latin Empire of Constantinople. There was no attempt to build castles during the failed attempts to conquer Thrace and north-western Anatolia. Instead, the invaders fortified some churches or took over existing Byzantine fortifications. During the initial invasion of Greece a small fort was erected at Pendeskouphi in the Crusader siege of 1205–10, but the primary role of castles was consolidation rather than conquest. Thereafter, wars between the Crusader States and the rival Byzantine rulers mostly consisted of raids, naval skirmishes, and small-scale sieges, with few major battles.

Bases for offensive operations

Following the fall of the last Crusader enclaves on the Middle Eastern mainland in 1291, fear spread of a Mamluk invasion of Cyprus. This threat failed to materialize, and instead Cyprus remained a Crusader base close to the heart of the Islamic world. While European fleets dominated the eastern Mediterranean, it needed little fortification. Instead, attempts were made to re-establish a

Girne (Kyrenia, Cyprus), known to medieval western Europeans as Cerina, showing the castle, inner harbour and the Turkish old town as they appeared in the 1950s.

bridgehead on the Syrian coast, to impose an economic blockade on the Mamluk Sultanate, and to support the Christian kingdom of Cilician Armenia.

Charles of Anjou, king of southern Italy, was the only major western monarch seriously interested in rolling back the Byzantine advances that overran so much Crusader territory in Greece during the mid 13th century – principally because he himself had ambitions in the area. Otherwise, the Castle of Thebes was built for Nicholas II de St Omer in 1287, at a time when the Crusaders of central Greece were returning to the offensive in southern Thessaly. The castle of Chastelneuf (possibly the site known as Veligosti), built around 1297, might have protected surrounding villages against Byzantine raiders from Gardiki, but this was built over 30 years earlier, so it is possible that Chastelneuf was actually part of a Crusader counter-offensive. An offensive strategy was clearer at Izmir (Smyrna), which was held by the Hospitallers from 1346 to 1402 and successfully crippled the previously threatening naval power of the Turkish *beylik* of Aydin.

Commercial outposts

The shortage of military manpower was particularly acute in the Italian colonial outposts, with around five local inhabitants of dubious loyalty for every one Venetian or Genoese. Theoretically, westerners lived inside walled towns dominated by a fortified *castrum* while locals inhabited the suburbs. In reality, however, many westerners also lived in the suburbs, although at Magusa in Cyprus there appears to have been a specifically Latin suburb close to the city walls.

Life in the Aegean was complicated by almost continuous naval conflicts following the Italian seizure of numerous islands in the aftermath of the Fourth Crusade. Many became meeting places for Christian pirates from all over the Mediterranean. Such pirates also had bases on the mainland coasts, and operating from here, or arriving as naval landing forces, they raided deep inland, sometimes capturing peasants for ransom or enslavement.

In a more peaceful vein the Crusader and Italian commercial outposts served as recruitment centres for local and foreign oarsmen seeking employment in the galleys. Skilled local pilots would also be available, while the ports themselves supplied food to passing ships, wine from Tenedos (probably sweet and red, like modern Mavrodafne), and dried figs from Foça (Phocea). Huge quantities of ships' biscuit were made in neighbouring countries like Bulgaria, and were then sold in bulk to ships that called at the major fortified harbours. Captured ships may also have been up for sale, though most were sold back to Italy. It is unclear whether prisoners-of-war were sold as slaves or, if they were fellow western European Christians, were sold to dealers who then extracted ransom from families or governments.

In 1386 only one or two large Venetian war-galleys were based at Corfu, two or four at Herakleion, one at Euboea, and one at Coron or Methoni, though there was also a larger number of smaller galliots. As the power of the Ottoman empire grew on land and at sea during the 15th century, some Venetian colonial fortifications, which had merely provided defence and refuge against pirates, now became major military and naval centres. Meanwhile, the Venetian government continued to foster good relations with the Ottoman Sultan through trade and negotiation wherever possible.

It is possible that a Turkish fleet from Aydin in the Aegean penetrated the Black Sea to attack Kiliya in the 1330s. Within a generation or so the Genoese outposts in this region were threatened not only by the Ottomans but also by the nearby Despot Dobrotitch, both of whom now had fleets. In contrast, the Genoese

The southern sea gate of Methoni (Modon), with the bridge and mole to the left. (Archive of the American School of Archaeology, Athens)

The southern end of the Acropolis of Athens. This part of the hilltop became a palace under Crusader rule, but the medieval structures were destroyed in the 19th century in an effort to return the site to its supposed Classical appearance. (Author's photograph)

fleet overcame a temporary threat by the Mongol Golden Horde to Genoese outposts on the northern coasts of the Black Sea, because the Mongols had no ships.

Bases for defensive operations

Defensive circumstances differed between regions. In Cyprus there was less urgency to modernize Byzantine fortifications, and little money to do so anyway. The only large new castle from the early period, overlooking Paphos, was to defend a strategic harbour, but it lost its importance after the Fourth Crusade. Destroyed by earthquake in 1222, it was subsequently used for building material. Other Cypriot fortifications upgraded in the early years were primarily to counter local Greek rebellion, but this danger also diminished after the Fourth Crusade. With a Byzantine revival in the mid 13th century, fear of an attempt to retake Cyprus resurfaced, but never seems to have reached a serious level.

One of the last additions that the Hospitallers made to their already powerful fortifications around the city of Rhodes was this artillery bastion, south of the medieval St George's Tower, which is visible in the background. (Author's photograph)

The restored 14th-and 15th-century walls of the Italian colonial outpost of Sudak (Soldaia) in the Crimea.

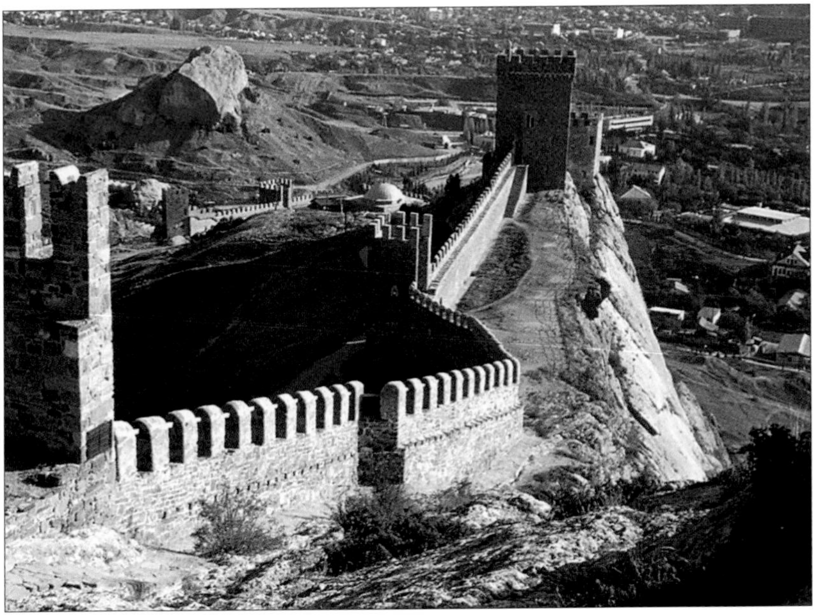

The disappearance of the Crusader States on the Middle Eastern mainland did, however, increase the threat of Islamic raiding, if not invasion. This became serious from the mid 14th century onwards and consequently harbour defences were the strongest type of fortification in Cyprus. Nevertheless, mountain-top citadels were more than mere refuges. St Hilarion overlooked the main pass between the port of Kyrenia and the capital of Nicosia, and in 1374 its garrison harassed Genoese supply columns during the siege of Kyrenia.

Greece was inhabited not only by settled Greek peasants and townsfolk, but also by sheep-raising semi-nomads. Most of these people did not speak Greek, and they dominated several mountainous regions. They also tended to raid the settled peoples of the plains – and were practically impossible for any government to control. In fact the Crusader States that emerged in the wake of the Fourth Crusade certainly did not truly 'rule' all the territory that appears as 'Crusader' in modern historical atlases. Many Crusader fortifications in Greece were probably designed to deal with these warlike tribal peoples, which included Albanians, Rumanian-speaking Vlachs, and Slavs such as the Melings of the Taygetos Mountains in the deep south of the Peloponnese. Mistra, Maina and Leuktron were apparently built for this purpose, and the location of Vardounia suggests that it had a similar role. There were usually two castles, one at each end of a vulnerable pass, but instead of serving as bases from which to attack the tribes in their own mountains, their garrisons usually attacked raiders as they returned laden with spoil and pursued by Crusader troops from the plains.

Mistra was the most important link in the defensive system established by William de Villehardouin, who chose this site, along with others, in 1249. According to P. Burridge:

> By examining the function of each castle and its relationship with its neighbours a picture of the medieval military strategy of the area begins to present itself. To the north the Langhada pass was protected at its western end by the castle of Kalamata and to the east by Mistra. Each castle also guaranteed the security of the productive plain in its vicinity. To the south the main pass between present-day Areopolis and Gytheion was guarded by Passava to the east and Oitylon/Kelefa to the west, the latter also protecting the principal harbour on the west coast. Any fortifications at

The Genoese fort at Çesme, on the Aegean coast of Turkey, was subsequently repaired by the Ottoman Turks. (Author's photograph)

Porto-Kayio and Tigani must have been designed to secure the anchorages adjacent to these sites. Zarnata – whenever it was built – as well as protecting the Kampos valley will have guarded the track southwards into the Mani. Control would also have been exercised over a rough, but passable, route from Anavryti (south of Mistra, on the eastern flanks of the Taygetos) to Kampos.[10]

Where the specific function of the Crusader castle of Beaufort was concerned, Burridge continues:

It would be remarkable if, after securing two of the major passes over the Taygetos, William failed to control the eastern side of the third pass either by strengthening an already existing defence or by building a new castle. To have built Beaufort without securing the eastern side of the pass would have left Beaufort and its fertile plain open to attack.

Although the Crusader States in Greece were in an almost constant state of war with one or other of their Byzantine neighbours, the chroniclers rarely mention castles being attacked. Having played virtually no role in the initial conquest, they did little more than slow down the subsequent Byzantine reconquests. The garrisons were not only tiny, but probably contained many Greeks whose loyalty to their Crusader rulers was shallow. As noted previously, in 1311 the castle of Thebes was surrendered to a marauding army of Catalan mercenaries after its field army had been defeated in open battle; the Catalans later destroyed it rather than let it fall into hands of Gautier II de Brienne.

The threat from the sea was perhaps more significant, though even here there was a tendency for garrisons to fight in the open before retreating within their walls. During the 13th century the main problem was caused by rivalry between Genoese, Pisans, Venetians, and Byzantines. Turkish-Islamic naval raiding increased in the 14th century. Several Crusader expeditions were launched in response, but had only a short-lived impact with the *beyliks* of Karasi, Saruhan, Mentese, and above all Aydin soon reviving to dominate much of the Aegean. Most Turkish fleets consisted of large numbers of small ships rather than the great war-galleys preferred by Christian naval powers. Turkish naval tactics also focussed on transporting men and horses as raiding parties – sometimes even carrying siege machines to attack coastal fortifications. Such fleets were very vulnerable to the large Christian galleys and tended to avoid

[10] Burridge, P. 'The Castle of Vardounia and the defence of the Southern Mani', in Lock, P. and Sanders, G.D.R. (eds.) *The Archaeology of Medieval Greece* (Oxford, 1996), 22.

combat at sea, enabling the Christian powers to claim 'naval domination', which, however, only existed when and where their war-galleys were present.

The Military Orders were active in defence of the Crusader States in Greece, initially against the Byzantines but later focussing on the Turks. In 1402 the Hospitallers twice sent their senior admiral, Buffilo Panizati, to inspect the defensive works being carried out at Izmir. The Christians had 20 years to strengthen this vital outpost and its garrison now consisted of 200 brother knights. The construction cost the Hospitallers a great deal of money, as did the maintainance of each knight in Izmir – nevertheless, the effort was considered worthwhile.

The main threat faced by the Venetian colonial authorities came from internal rebellion in Crete and savage guerrilla warfare. Then came the Ottoman Turks' combined army and naval campaign that conquered Euboea (Negroponte) in 1470. This was a terrible shock to the Italians who had, until then, not feared the Ottoman fleet. By that date the remnants of the Crusader States had already fallen, but, being on the mainland, they had been overrun by the Ottoman army, not the navy. Small wonder that Venice, which took over Cyprus in 1489, concentrated on defending its coast while largely abandoning inland castles, many of which were dismantled.

The Genoese outposts in the Crimea faced different problems. Here the Italian colonial governors controlled a long but narrow coastal strip, which was backed by ranges of mountains that lay between the fortified ports and the steppe Khanates of the interior. These mountains were also the powerbase of a little-known, essentially Byzantine Christian people who maintained their own series of fortresses, some carved from the mountain rock itself. Nevertheless, the vaste Mongol Khanate of the Golden Horde remained the dominant land power in this region, and it was the temporarily anti-Christian policy adopted by its ruler that caused the Genoese to refortify Kaffa in 1313.

The fortifications under attack

Until the arrival of the Ottomans, armies in late medieval Greece tended to be small with little siege equipment. During the 13th century the Crusader States' most pressing enemy was the revived Byzantine 'Empire of Nicea', which subsequently re-established itself as the main, though not the only, claimant to be *the* Byzantine Empire. The Despotate of Mistra in southern Greece formed part of this revived empire and was a constant threat to the Crusader Principality of Achaea. Until the mid 14th century its armies were very mixed, including many Western mercenaries as well as Turks, Albanians, and local tribal forces.

These were effective in open warfare but their siege capabilities are virtually unknown. According to the *Chronicle of the Morea*, the Byzantine 'Grand Domestikos' senior army commander considered attacking the castle of Andravida after being defeated in a skirmish, but a European mercenary advised trying to lure the Crusader Prince William into the open:

> I have learned that the prince has returned to Andravida and that the armies that he brought have gone home; let us go straight to him there in Andravida; and if he should have such misfortune as to come out to battle, do not set to fighting him with arrogance, but only fighting him with skill and cunning.[11]

However, those who knew this area well advised the Byzantine commander not to go to Andravida 'because the approaches were too narrow for the balistas [*tzagratoros*, crossbows] and their crews'. After an inconclusive skirmish the Byzantines withdrew and the Grand Domestikos instead besieged the castle of Nikli, where his Turkish mercenaries changed sides because they had not been

[11] Anon (tr. Lurier, H.E.) *Chronicle of the Morea, Crusaders as Conquerors* (New York, 1964), 218.

The castle of Sathines (Athens Acropolis) in the late 14th century

The world famous Parthenon Temple on the Acropolis (upper city) of Athens had been converted into a Christian church in the 6th century; it served as the cathedral of the Crusader Duchy of Athens from 1208 to 1458. However, virtually every fragment of post-Classical architecture on the Acropolis was removed during the 19th century in an almost fanatical attempt to recreate what had existed in the Golden Age of Classical Greece. This meant that not only the Ottoman Turkish mosque, houses and other structures were demolished, but also what remained from the Byzantine and Crusader periods. One of the last items to go was a tall stone tower (1), similar to those that still dot the countryside of Attica. It survived long enough to be photographed and had at least one overhanging box-machicolation (2) above its only entrance door.

Facing it, the north wing of the Propylaea or main entrance complex of the ancient Acropolis (3) had been raised in height and was used as the chancellery of the Duchy of Athens. When the Italian banker Nerio Acciaioli Lord of Corinth became duke of Athens in 1388 he converted the Propylaea into a fine Italian-style palace known as the Mnesikles. Acciaioli is also sometimes credited with constructing the fortified tower. To what extent the rest of the site was fortified remains unknown, though crenellated walls (4) were built around various parts of the ancient Acropolis, and fallen drums of ancient columns were often used as defences or obstructions in subsequent fortifications (5). Serious defences were certainly added during the Ottoman period. In the 17th century the palace, which was currently being used as the Ottoman governor's residence, was struck by lightning; a magazine exploded and part of the Classical portico collapsed.

paid. Half a century later the Byzantine army proved much more effective and in 1316 Andonikos Asen, the emperor's governor in the Peloponnese, defeated the Crusaders' field army in open battle near the castle of St George – though again the fortress itself played only a minimal role.

Events concerning minor fortifications and isolated towers were usually too insignificant to warrant mention in the chronicles. Nevertheless, the people of the Archangelos area of Rhodes petitioned the Hospitaller Grand Master for a small castle in 1399 because of the increasing danger of naval raids. Instead, they were permitted to seek refuge in the existing castle of Feraklos five kilometres away. Some time after 1399 a castle was constructed at Archangelos but was stormed with ease by the Ottomans in 1457. Thirteen years earlier the citadel of Lindos was more successful in sheltering the inhabitants when a substantial Mamluk army invaded Rhodes. In 1395 the whole population of the island of Leros retreated into the castle every night for fear of raiders.

Most early Ottoman conquests in Greece and the Balkans were achieved by persistent raiding and once the surrounding countryside had been subdued, the remaining fortified places eventually came to terms with the Ottoman invaders. Only coastal enclaves, resupplied by ship, could withstand such tactics, but once the Turks took to the seas they too came under serious threat. To make matters worse, the local Greek island populations were often hostile to their Latin-Catholic rulers and frequently helped the Muslim Turks.

Seen from the Muslim perspective, however, the garrisons of Crusader castles could seem large and remarkably well equipped, especially when Turkish naval raiders lacked cavalry. The Turkish epic *Destan of Umur Pasha* describes one such attack on Chios: 'The Franks numbered ten thousand, all covered in iron they came to give combat,' and emerged to fight the raiders in open battle. The major role of crossbows in defence of Christian fortification is reflected in another Turkish epic, the *Danishmand-name*, which survives in a mid 14th century form. These weapons apparently included frame-mounted versions, which were used alongside stone-throwing mangonels, Greek-fire incendiary devices, simple fire-arrows, and the *tufenk*, which was an early form of musket.

The southern curtain wall and gate of the outer enceinte of Old Navarino (Palaia Avarino), looking west. It was called Chastel du Port de Junch by the Crusaders. (Archive of the American School of Archaeology, Athens)

The citadel and town walls of Soldaia (Sudak, Crimea) in the 15th century

Today Soldaia is the best-preserved medieval fortified city on the Crimean coast, though it was not the most important during the period of Genoese rule. Its fortifications were made of red sandstone and much of these have been restored in modern times. The oldest part of the defences was probably a simple Byzantine tower on the top of the hill (1), but the line and perhaps the foundations of the curtain walls (2) might also date from the Byzantine period. The summits of at least two of the larger towers were decorated with rows of blind arches in what would seem to have been an Italian fashion (3). Many of the smaller rectangular towers were much simpler, being partially open at the back (4) and with wooden floors, in a style common in Byzantine, Balkan, and some early Ottoman military architecture. There also seems to have been a group of substantial towers or fortified structures where the land walls met those facing the sea, perhaps creating a strongly defended entrance complex (5). How much of the interior of the walled town was built up with commercial premises, houses, orchards, and gardens (6) is unclear. Outside the walled town there were also suburbs or scattered houses.

The most catastrophic siege was Timur-i Lenk's (Tamerlane's) assault on Izmir (Smyrna) in 1402. While Timur's troops ravaged the area, largely focussing on Turkish rather than Christian-held localities, preparations continued in Izmir. The defences were concentrated on the rugged peninsula, which included a castle that 'closed' the port and was separated from the mainland by a recently excavated deep ditch. Izmir was, in fact, thought impregnable and the Hospitaller garrison felt confident. Munitions, food supplies, money, and troops continued to arrive. Timur led his own 'central' army towards Izmir on 2 December 1402, where his left and right 'flank' armies were ordered to join him. Almost immediately his siege machines and miners set to work on several parts of the fortifications. Timur also ordered a senior officer to construct a massive platform on wooden piles to stop enemy ships entering the port. A few days later the armies of the left and right wings joined the siege. Timur now ordered a full-scale bombardment, which survivors compared to a 'Second Deluge'. After two days Timur's miners weakened a stretch of the outer walls; the props were burned, the wall collapsed, and a general assault swept into Izmir. Resistance was scattered; the Hospitaller knights fled to their ships, and the population was slaughtered while several ships, which had come to support the city, turned and fled, fearing Timur's stone-throwing machines. Meanwhile, the nearby Genoese outpost at Foça (Old Phocaea) surrendered, following the example of Yeni Foça (New Phocea), which had sent a peace ambassador to Timur. When Francesco II Gattilusio, the Genoese ruler of Lesbos, also surrendered and, like the Genoese authorities on Chios, offered to pay tribute, Timur-i Lenk won temporary control over two large Aegean islands – without launching a single warship.

Western historians have tended to dismiss the Mamluk Sultanate of Egypt and Syria as having little interest in naval affairs. This is not true, as those on the receiving end of several Mamluk attacks could testify. However, such assaults were raids in force rather than attempts at conquest. One of the most effective took place during the reign of the Sultan al-Ashraf Barsbey and was in retaliation for Cypriot piracy against Mamluk merchant vessels.

In 1424 five ships, two of which were brigandines with 80 elite Mamluk soldiers on board, set out from Cairo down the Nile. At Dumyat (Damietta) they were joined by a galley manned by Egyptian volunteers. Two more ships joined the fleet at Beirut and Sidon, substantially increasing the number of troops

BELOW The rocky summit of the Crusader castle at Livadia in central Greece. (Author's photograph)

The citadel and town walls of Soldaia (Sudak, Crimea) in the 15th century

The castle of Bilhorod-Dnistrovsky on the Black Sea coast of Ukraine was called Moncastro in the late medieval period. It was also known as Cetatea Alba in Romanian and Ak-Kirman in Turkish.

involved. They reached the Cypriot coast south of Limassol where they captured a Christian merchant ship whose crew had fled as they approached. After looting then burning this vessel, the Mamluk fleet sailed to Limassol. King Janus of Cyprus had been warned of their approach, so the Muslim squadron was met by three fully armed warships, but these were soon defeated and burned. As soon as they landed, the raiders were attacked by the vanguard of the Cypriot army, which they again drove off, killing its commander, Philippe de Picquingni. After raiding the area, the Mamluks considered attacking the castle of Limassol, but, lacking siege equipment, they instead sailed towards Paphos, capturing one and burning a second enemy galley on their way. After devastating the region of Kouklia, they returned home him with one captured galley, 23 prisoners for ransom, and considerable booty.[12]

On this occasion the fortifications as Limassol had done what they were supposed to do, but the limitations of such urban defences became apparent during the next Mamluk raid in 1425. This involved eight Mamluk vessels from Egypt supported by smaller ships from Lebanon carrying volunteers. Eventually the fleet, commanded by Jirbash al-Karimi, consisted of five large war-galleys, 19 smaller galleys, six horse transports, and 12 galliots. It set sail from Tripoli on 30 July. Genoese-held Magusa surrendered immediately, raising the Sultan's flag on 4 August. The Genoese also provided information about Cypriot defences. Next came a full-scale naval battle within sight of Larnaca, which the Muslim fleet won, after which the Mamluks ravaged a wide area. On 15 August they landed a mere 150 men, who stormed Limassol town and castle with relative ease after escaped Muslim slaves told them about a poorly guarded stretch of wall. Nevertheless, news now arrived that the Venetians were sending substantial support to the Cypriot king, who had also assembled a large army to attack the raiders. So the Mamluks abandoned Limassol, defeated the Cypriot army in several small skirmishes, then sailed home with much more booty than before and over a thousand prisoners.

Gunpowder artillery was now having a major influence upon both defence and attack. In fact the Venetian fortifications in Greece, including those at Methoni, Korone and Nauphlia, are amongst the best examples from this period. Until 1470 the Venetians had continued the medieval reliance on height, but this gave way to lower, thicker earth-filled ramparts with broad *terrepleines* on top for cannon. The earliest-dated Venetian artillery constructions

---

[12] Ziada, M.M. 'The Mamluk conquest of Cyprus in the fifteenth century (part 1)', *Bulletin of the Faculty of Arts, Cairo University*, 1 (1933), 93–4.

The entrance to the keep of Chlemutzi (Clairmont, or Castel Tornese) castle (right) and directly ahead a postern gate through the enceinte. (Ian Meigh)

are those designed by Vettore Pasqualigo at Nauphlia. They were primarily designed to face Ottoman Turkish attack, but even before this the struggles between rival Christian powers in late medieval Greece, including Catalans and Aragonese, might be reflected in the deeply anti-Genoese, Catalan epic *Tirant lo Blanc*. This was written in the mid 15th century. In one description of the defence of a castle, the hero Tirant orders that a bulwark be built inside the gate, which was itself left open. When the enemy charged in they were trapped and killed. Fearing enemy mining beneath the walls, Tirant also ordered countermines to be dug and filled with brass bowls, which rattled when enemy miners used pickaxes. Next the enemy tried to attack through these tunnels, but Tirant fired bombards into the entrances.

The north-eastern tower of the citadel (now the İç Kale) of the Genoese fortified outpost of Amasra on the Black Sea coast of Turkey. It appears to be the only round tower in the entire defensive system. (Author's photograph)

Though fictitious and exaggerated, Tirant's adventures probably reflected reality. The first unsuccessful Ottoman siege of Hospitaller-held Rhodes in 1480 was, however, brutally real. Sultan Mehmet tried to keep news of his fleet's departure secret, but the Grand Master had an effective intelligence network and was able to get the local inhabitants and their animals inside various castles before the Turks arrived. The small Hospitaller fleet did not challenge the enemy at sea, but allowed them to establish a bridgehead almost unopposed. The Ottomans then attempted to take the city of Rhodes at a rush, but failed. Next the Turks bombarded the Tower of St Nicholas, which protected the shallower Mandraki or northern harbour. This resulted in a duel between three large Ottoman mangonels in the garden and orchard of the Church of St Anthony, hurling stones across the Mandraki harbour, and three Hospitaller bombards in the garden of the Inn of Auvergne (the hostel of Hospitaller brothers from central France). Subsequently the Turks established several other mangonel and cannon batteries, the struggle continuing to focus on the vulnerable Tower of St Nicholas throughout June and most of July. In fact this tower was badly damaged, though the Hospitaller defenders constructed a timber stockade to protect the damaged sections.

After unsuccessfully attacking the Tower of St Nicholas from the sea, the Turks tried to anchor a pontoon supported by barrels across the Mandraki harbour. This enabled them to take the mole and isolate the tower, but the pontoon's mooring ropes were cut by swimmers at night. Part of the Turkish fleet now sailed into the Mandraki and bombarded the tower while the pontoon was towed back into position, followed by an assault. But the defenders' artillery destroyed many of the attackers' boats and eventually the Ottoman attack on Rhodes was abandoned after another assault on the other side of the town failed. It would be another 42 years before Sultan Mehmet's grandson, Sulaiman the Magnificent, finally conquered Rhodes in 1522.

Aftermath

Several Crusader castles in Greece lost their strategic significance after being reconquered by the Byzantines, but, being distant from major towns, were not pillaged as sources of building material – as happened to the Castle of Forty Columns in Cyprus. Consequently these Greek castles remained virtually unchanged. Other fortified locations of Crusader origin remained important or even increased in military significance. The most famous was Mistra, which became the capital of the Byzantine Despotate in the Peloponnese. Its superb late Byzantine churches and their wall paintings date from this later Byzantine period. Mistra remained locally important under Ottoman Turkish rule, the castle again being slightly altered while several charming but now utterly ruined Islamic buildings were added to the town. The greatest damage to Mistra occurred in the 19th century, when it was burned and then devastated by Russians and Albanians.

The Byzantine Despots of Mistra also modified several other inland Crusader castles, while the coastal fortresses were even more substantially altered by the Venetians. For example, the existing castle of Vardounia incorporates elements from many different periods, both before and after the introduction of gunpowder. Alterations from the age of firearms are mostly visible on the highest parts of existing structure, though in fact the walls and towers were probably higher in the Crusader era than in subsequent centuries.

Constantine Palaiologos, the Despot of Mistra and subsequently the last Byzantine emperor, took up residence at Clairmont in 1427. In 1430 he destroyed the Crusader castle of Clarence (Clarenza) and, perhaps, the neighbouring town, while his army may also have devastated Beauvoir (Pontikocastro). It has, however, been suggested that the present castle of Clairmont is not actually a Crusader structure at all, but was built by Constantine Palaiologos to replace the Crusader castle that he destroyed some distance away. Having been regained by

This 13th-century tower is virtually all that remains of the once luxurious Crusader castle of Kadmeia at Thebes. (Author's photograph)

Platamon (Pandeleimon) castle, built between 1204 and 1222 with later additions. It is one of the best-preserved Crusader castles in central Greece. (Author's photograph)

the Byzantines from the Latins in 1429, Patras was certainly rebuilt during this period in a final effort by Constantine to stem the Ottoman advance. In the event the castle of Patras did hold out when the Turks first took the town, obliging them to retreat. Only in 1458 did both the town and the castle of Patras surrender to Sultan Mehmet the Conqueror.

The fate of those of western European origin and Catholic religion who had held Crusader castles in Greece was varied. As the Latins lost territory to Byzantine reconquest, the senior aristocracy was either killed or returned to France or Italy. Lower-ranking members of Crusader society found it more difficult to leave, many migrating to the Venetian colonies or being absorbed into the Byzantine military elite. In southern Greece many families were clearly assimilated in this way, and became loyal military supporters of the Byzantine empire. Whether they retained any connection with the ex-Crusader fortifications is unknown, as is the fate of their descendants under Turkish rule. Many were probably incorporated into the Ottoman military system, along with so many of the Byzantine military class.

The Ottoman impact upon castles of Crusader origin was similarly varied. During the early decades the Turks strengthened some fortifications, but most were now irrelevant and were consequently abandoned. Where the early Ottomans did make changes, these were mostly a continuation of Byzantine military architectural trends, although stronger towers in the Arab-Islamic tradition were added to incorporate or resist firearms.

Genoese outposts in the Aegean survived slightly longer than those around the Black Sea. Although the Ottoman Sultans were more sympathetic towards Orthodox Christians, especially Greeks, than towards Latin or western Catholics, they allowed the Genoese Gattilusi to retain control of Lemnos under Ottoman suzerainty following the fall of Constantinople. This was probably when the Gattilusi added gun emplacements to Myrina Kastro, strong enough to bear the weight and recoil of modern firearms, though these may also be later Ottoman Turkish improvements. After several years of chaos and oppression the local Greeks appealed to the Sultan, who handed the island to a member of the ex-Byzantine imperial family in 1457. Finally, in 1467, Ottoman direct rule was imposed, though the Venetians continued to dispute the island until 1478. Thereafter there was little need for fortifications, as the Aegean Sea was now

The hilltop fortifications of Acrocorinth (Corinth), showing the keep and east wall of the redoubt, built by the Villehardouin dynasty in the 13th century. (Archive of the American School of Archaeology, Athens)

effectively an Ottoman lake. The Gattilusi rulers of Lesbos paid tribute to the Sultan until 1462 and the Genoese *Mahone* on Chios survived as late as 1566, the same year that the Sultan gave the ex-Crusader island and Duchy of Naxos to the famous Jewish governor, Joseph Nasi.

The fate of the Venetian outposts tended to be more clearcut. At Monemvasia, most of the Crusader and Byzantine fortifications were on the summit, forming an acropolis. Under later Venetian rule these were abandoned and a new town called Ghefira was built on the shore, within Venetian fortifications that extended from the acropolis to the sea. However, much of the existing urban walls date from the first Ottoman and second Venetian periods in the later 16th to early 18th centuries. The fort of Palamede at Nauphlia was similarly rebuilt by the Venetians in 1711, virtually enclosing the Crusader structures within new ones designed to resist modern artillery.

The Ottomans took and garrisoned the island fortress of Giurgiu in the River Danube in 1394, and 50 years later the ex-Genoese enclave of Kiliya on the Black Sea coast was occupied by Hungary's local allies. Twenty or so years after the Ottoman conquest of Istanbul, all the Genoese outposts around the Black Sea had fallen, and in the end Kaffa sought protection from Poland – but this also failed. Most of the local inhabitants refused to fight for Genoa and instead made terms with the Ottomans, who took control in 1479. The fall of Kaffa led to a brief attempt at a Genoese–Moldavian alliance against the Ottoman empire, and the same year Steven the Great of Moldavia sent a force of 800 masons and over 17,000 labourers to strengthen the defences of Kiliya. Only Kiliya and Moncastro (Bilhorod-Dnistrovsky) now remained, but their Moldavian garrisons surrendered to a major Ottoman land and sea campaign in 1484.

Visiting the fortifications today

Fortifications associated with the Crusaders and their Italian trading allies outside the Middle East are generally easy to reach, though sometimes well off the beaten track. Political problems only interfere in Cyprus, while the emergence of the Ukraine as an independent state has largely removed the problems previously associated with independent travel within the Soviet Union.

Cyprus

Almost all the medieval fortifications on Cyprus are easily accessible. However, some are located in the Greek south and others in the Turkish north of the island. Both 'states' have well-developed tourist industries, hotel accommodation of all grades, and efficient transport systems. What is missing is an open frontier between the two, which in reality means that separate trips are probably needed if castles on both sides of the divide are to be seen.

Greece

Greece has all the facilities required by a major tourist destination. Unfortunately, Greek 'cultural tourism' has concentrated on the country's Classical past, with

LEFT An internal passage with archery embrasures, inside one of the walls of Kantara (Le Candare) castle in Cyprus. (Marion Youden)

RIGHT The gate of the castle of Karytaina in southern Greece. (A. Bon)

some attention also being given to its Byzantine heritage. Relics from the medieval Crusader period are largely neglected, while the Ottoman heritage sometimes seems to be deliberately hidden from view. Several Crusader castles are actually more closely associated with the Turks than with the 'Latins', and are thus not made easily accessible. Furthermore, most Crusader fortifications are well off the normal tourist routes – in several cases off any routes whatsoever. So those wishing to visit them are almost obliged to hire a sturdy self-drive car, motorbike, or bicycle, and then to expect a hard walk or climb to follow.

The arms of Genoa flanked by those of two of the Genoese families that dominated this trading post, carved on the fortified walls of Amasra on the Black Sea. (Author's photograph)

Turkey

Like Greece, those coastal parts of Turkey where Crusader and medieval Italian colonial fortifications exist have a fully developed tourist trade. The Crusader fortifications on Turkey's Aegean coast have, in fact, become major features of their regional tourist industries. The Black Sea coast is less known to European visitors, but has good hotels and transport facilities, which largely cater for Turkish rather than foreign visitors.

Ukraine

The Crimean peninsula was a favourite vacation area within the former Soviet Union, and its magnificent southern coast was provided with numerous, if huge and rather barracks-like, hotels. These still exist and the Ukrainian authorities are now modernizing the old Soviet tourism infrastructure. The superb medieval walled city of Sudak, the Soldaia of the Genoese and Venetians, was one of the jewels of Crimean tourism and is likely to regain its reputation in the future. The western end of Ukraine's Black Sea coast is low-lying and less scenic, primarily being of interest to bird-watchers and those wanting to visit the remarkable fortress of Bilhorod-Dnistrovsky. Unfortunately this is quite close to the disputed Moldovan territory of the self-proclaimed Transnistrian Republic, while the nearest 'listed' hotels are in the city of Odessa, a hundred kilometres away.

59

Modern names and country[13]	Medieval western European names
Agriosikia (Tilos, Greece)	
Akçaabat (Turkey)	
Akova (Greece)	Matagrifon
Amasra (Turkey)	Amastris
Anamur (Turkey)	Stallimuri
Androusa (Greece)	
Argos (Greece)	Argos
Athens Acropolis (Greece)	Sathines
Beskapilar [Foça] (Turkey)	Phocaea
Bilhorod-Dnistrovsky (Ukraine)	Moncastro
Bodonitsa (Greece)	Medietas Bondonicie
Bodrum (Turkey)	Castrum Sancti Petri
Boudonitsa (Greece)	
Buffavento (Cyprus)	Bufevent
Çandarli (Turkey)	
Chalkis (Greece)	Negroponte
Chanea (Greece)	Canea
Chlemutzi (Greece)	Clairmont/Castel Tornese
Clarenza (Greece)	Clarence
Corinth (Greece)	Corinth
Dafni (Greece)	Daphne
Galata (Istanbul, Turkey)	Pera
Gardiki (Greece)	Gardiki
Gastria (Cyprus)	Gastria
Geraki (Greece)	Geraki
Giresun (Turkey)	
Girne [Kyrenia] (Cyprus)	Cerina
Herakleion (Greece)	Candia
Izmit (Turkey)	Nicomedia
Kaffa (Ukraine)	Caffa
Kalamata (Greece)	Kalamata
Kalavryta (Greece)	Tremola
Kantara (Cyprus)	Le Candare
Karytaina (Greece)	Karytaina
Kelafa [Oitylon] (Greece)	Grand Magne
Khirokitia (Cyprus)	
Kiliya (Ukraine)	Licostomo/Kilia
Kolossi (Cyprus)	Le Colos
Korikos (Turkey)	Corycus
Korone (Greece)	Coron
Kotsinas (Lemnos, Greece)	
Kyparissa (Greece)	Arkadia
Kyrenia (Cyprus)	Kyrenia
Lamia (Greece)	Zeitoun/Ravennika
Larissa (Greece)	Larisa

Modern names and country (contd.)[13]	Medieval western European names (contd.)
Lebadeia (Greece)	Levadia
Leuktron (Greece)	Beaufort
Limassol (Cyprus)	Limassol
Lindos (Rhodos, Greece)	Lindos
Livadia (Greece)	Levadia
Magusa [Famagusta] (Cyprus)	Famagusta
Megalo Horio (Tilos, Greece)	
Methoni (Greece)	Modon
Methymna (Lesbos, Greece)	Molivos
Meyisti (Greece)	Kastellorizo
Mistra (Greece)	Mistras
Monemvasia (Greece)	Napoli di Malvasia
Monolithos (Rhodos, Greece)	
Myrina Kastro [Lemnos] (Greece)	Lemnos
Myteleni (Lesbos, Greece)	Mitilini
Nauphlia (Greece)	Napoli di Romania
Navarino [Palaia Avarino] (Greece)	Chastel du Port de Junch
Neopatras (Greece)	Lepater
Nicosia/Lefkosa (Cyprus)	Nicosia
Palaiokastro (Lemnos, Greece)	
Pandeleimon (Greece)	Platamon
Paphos (Cyprus)	Paphos
Parga (Greece)	
Patras (Greece)	Patras
Pendeskupi (Greece)	
Pontikocastro [Katakolo] (Greece)	Beauvoir (Belvedere)
Ravennika (Greece)	
Rhodes (Greece)	Rhodes
Salona (Greece)	
Silifke (Turkey)	Selef
Sivouri (Cyprus)	
St George (Greece)	
St Hilarion (Cyprus)	Dieudamour
Sudak (Ukraine)	Soldaia
Sykaminon (Greece)	
Thebes, castle of (Greece)	Kadmeia
Tirebolu (Turkey)	
Vardounia (Greece)	(possibly Passavant)
Veligosti (Greece)	(possibly Chastelneuf)
Vordonia (Greece)	Verdognia (Verdonia)
Vostitza (Greece)	
Yermasoyia (Cyprus)	
Zarnata (Greece)	(possibly Gerenia)
Zeitoun (Greece)	Lamia

[13] This listing excludes the numerous rural towers in Greece and the fortified farmsteads around Venetian-ruled Messenia. For more comprehensive lists of these towers see the following works: P. Lock 'The Frankish Towers of Central Greece', *The Annual of the British School at Athens*, 81 (1986) 101–23; 'The Medieval Towers of Greece: A Problem of Chronology and Function', in B. Arbel, B. Hamilton & D. Jacoby (eds.) *Latins and Greeks in the Eastern Mediterranean after 1204* (London 1989) 129–45; 'The Towers of Euboea: Lombard or Venetian, Agrarian or Strategic', in P. Lock & G.D.R. Sanders (eds.) *The Archaeology of Medieval Greece* (Oxford 1996) 107–26. For the fortified farmsteads around the Gulf of Messenia see: C. Hodgetts & P. Lock 'Some Village Fortification in the Venetian Peloponnese', in P. Lock & G.D.R. Sanders (eds.) *The Archaeology of Medieval Greece* (Oxford 1996) 77–90.

Further reading

Andrews, K. *Castles of the Morea* (Princeton, 1953).

Anghel, G. 'Les fortéresses moldaves de l'époque d'Etienne le Grand', *Château Gaillard,* 7 (1975), 21–34.

Balard, M. 'Les formes militaires de la colonisation Génoise (XIIIe–XVe siècles)', *Castrum,* 3 (Madrid, 1988), 67–78.

Beldiceanu, N. 'La conquête des cités marchandes de Kilia et de Cetatea Alba par Bayezid II', *Südost-Forschungen,* 22 (1964), 36–90.

Blin, R. 'Châteaux croisés de Grèce: Fortifications franques de Morée', *Histoire Médiévale,* 56 (August 2004), 58–67.

Bon, A. 'Forteresses médiévales de la Grèce centrale,' *Bulletin de Correspondence Hellénique,* 61 (1937), 136–209.

Bon, A. *La Morée franque* (Paris, 1969).

Burridge, P. 'The Castle of Vardounia and Defence in the Southern Mani', in Lock, P. and Sanders, G.D.R. (eds.) *The Archaeology of Medieval Greece* (Oxford, 1996), 19–28.

Crow, J. and Hill, S. 'Amasra, a Byzantine and Genoese Fortress', *Fortress,* 15 (1990), 3–13.

Elliott, R. 'Lemnos and its Castle', *Fortress,* 17 (1993), 28–36.

Fedden, R. *Crusader Castles: A Brief Study in the Military Architecture of the Crusades* (London, 1950).

Fiene, E. *Die Burg von Kyrenia* (Hannover, 1993).

Fiene, E. *St. Hilarion, Buffavento, Kantara: Bergburgen in Nordzypern* (Hannover, 1992).

Gertwagen, R. 'Venetian Modon and its Port (1358–1500)', in Cowan, A. (ed.) *Mediterranean Urban Culture 1400–1700* (Exeter, 2000), 128–48.

Gertwagen, R. 'The Venetian Colonies in the Ionian Sea and the Aegean in Venetian Defence Policy in the Fifteenth Century', *Journal of Mediterranean Studies,* 12 (2002), 351–84.

Hodgetts, C. and Lock, P. 'Some Village Fortifications in the Venetian Peloponnese', in Lock, P. and Sanders, G.D.R. (eds.) *The Archaeology of Medieval Greece* (Oxford, 1996), 77–90.

Jeffery, G.H. *Cyprus Monuments: Historical and Architectural Buildings* (Nicosia, 1937).

Karasava-Tsilingiri, F. 'Fifteenth Century Hospitaller Architecture on Rhodes: Patrons and Master Builders', in Nicholson, H. (ed.) *The Military Orders, Volume 2: Welfare and Warfare* (Aldershot, 1998), 259–65.

Lock, P. 'Castles and Seigneurial Influence in Latin Greece', in Murray, A.V. (ed.) *From Clermont to Jerusalem: The Crusades and Crusader Societies 1095–1500* (Turnhout, 1998), 173–86.

Lock, P. 'The Frankish Tower on the Acropolis, Athens; the Photographs of William J. Stillman', *Annual of the British School at Athens,* 82 (1987), 131–33 (pls. 46–8).

Lock, P. 'The Frankish Towers of Central Greece', *Annual of the British School of Archaeology at Athens,* 81 (1986), 101–23.

Lock, P. 'The Medieval Towers of Greece: A Problem of Chronology and Function', in Arbel, B., Hamilton, B. and Jacoby, D. (eds.) *Latins and Greece in the Eastern Mediterranean after 1204* (London, 1989), 129–45.

Lock, P. 'The Towers of Euboea: Lombard or Venetian, Agrarian or Strategic?' in Lock, P. and Sanders, G.D.R. (eds.) *The Archaeology of Medieval Greece* (Oxford, 1996), 107–26.

Lock, P. 'Castles of Frankish Greece', in Murray, A. (ed.) *From Clermont to Jerusalem: The Crusades and Crusader Societies* (Brepols, 1997).

Lurier, H.E. (tr.) *Crusaders as Conquerors: The Chronicle of the Morea* (New York, 1964).

Luttrell, A. 'English Contributions to the Hospitaller Castle at Bodrum in Turkey; 1407–1437', in Nicholson, H. (ed.) *The Military Orders, Volume 2: Welfare and Warfare* (Aldershot, 1998), 163–72.

Luttrell, A. 'Lindos and the Defence of Rhodes; 1306–1522', *Rivista di Studi Byzantini e Neoellenici*, 22–3 (1985–86), 317–32.

Luttrell, A. 'The Later History of the Maussolleion and its Utilization in the Hospitaller Castle at Bodrum', *Jutland Archaeological Society Publications*, 15 (1986), 117–222.

Megaw, P. 'A Castle in Cyprus Attributable to the Hospital?' in Barber, M. (ed.) *The Military Orders: Fighting for the Faith and Caring for the Sick* (Aldershot, 1994), 42–51.

Megaw, A.H.S. 'The Arts of Cyprus, B: Military Architecture', in Hazard, H.W. and Setton, K.M. (eds.) *A History of the Crusades, Volume 4: The Art and Architecture of the Crusader States* (Madison, 1977), 196–207.

Megaw, A.H.S. 'Supplementary Excavations on a Castle Site at Paphos, Cyprus, 1970–1971,' *Dumbarton Oaks Papers*, 26 (1972), 322–45.

Molin, K. 'Fortifications and Internal Security in the Kingdom of Cyprus, 1191–1426', in Morray, A.V. (ed.) *From Clermont to Jerusalem: The Crusades and Crusader Societies 1095–1500* (Turnhout, 1998), 187–99.

Molin, K. *Unknown Crusader Castles* (London, 2001).

Müller-Wiener, W. *Castles of the Crusaders* (London, 1966).

Paradissis, A. *Fortresses and Castles of Greece* (Athens & Thessaloniki, 1972–82).

Rosser, J. 'Crusader Castles of Cyprus', *Archaeology*, 39/4 (July–August 1986), 40–7.

Rosser, J. 'Excavations at Saranda Kolones, Paphos, Cyprus, 1981–1983', *Dumbarton Oaks Papers*, 39 (1985), 80–97.

Rubio y Lluch, A. 'Els castells catalans de la Grècia continentale', *Annuari de l'Institut d'estudis catalans*, 2 (1908), 364–425.

Sort, R. 'Two Hospitaller Castles on the Island of Tilos, on the Southern Dodecanese (Megalo Horio & Agriosikia)', *Castles Studies Group, Newsletter*, 15 (2001–02), 96–100.

Traquair, R. 'Frankish Architects in Greece', *Journal of the Royal Institute of British Architects*, 31 (1923–24), 33–48 and 73–86.

Traquair, R. 'Laconia, I: Medieval Fortresses', *Annual of the British School at Athens*, 12 (1905–06), 259–76 (pls. II–VI).

Traquair, R. 'Medieval Fortresses of the North-Western Peloponnesus', *Annual of the British School at Athens*, 13 (1906–07), 268–84 (pls. VIII–IX).

Ziada, M.M. 'The Mamluk Conquest of Cyprus in the Fifteenth Century' (two parts), *Bulletin of the Faculty of Arts, Cairo University*, 1 (1933), 90–113; 2 (1934), 37–57.

Glossary

antemurabilus   Second or outer walls.

ashlar   Stone cut into rectangular blocks and laid in rows.

bailey, bailli   Fortified enclosure within a castle.

barbican   Outer defensive enclosure of a castle or city, usually outside a gate.

barrel vault   Vaulting in the form of an elongated arch.

bastion   Projecting or additional part of a fortification.

batter   Slope, usually on the outer face, of a fortified wall.

boulevard   Low and extended platform to form an artillery emplacement in front of a fortified wall.

bretéche   Projecting machicolation above a gate.

casemate   Covered emplacement for cannon.

castrum (pl: **castra**)   Fortified enclosure, usually rectangular.

chatelain   Commander of a castle.

chemin de ronde   Raised walkway around the curtain walls of a fortified place.

concentric castle   Fortification with two or more circuit walls within each other.

corbel   Stone bracket to support another structure.

counterfort, counter-tower   Fortification, usually small, to blockade or isolate another fortification.

cour d'honneur   Central or ceremonial court of a castle-palace.

crenellation   Tooth-like projection along the top of a fortified wall to provide protection for the defenders as well as spaces through which they can observe or shoot.

curtain wall   Continuous defensive wall around a fortified location.

donjon   Main tower of a fortified location.

drawbridge   Entrance bridge, usually over a moat, which can be raised, usually blocking the gate behind.

embossed masonry   Blocks of stone in which the centre is left raised and usually roughly cut.

embrasure   Opening in a fortified wall, tower, crenellation or other structure through which the defenders can shoot.

enceinte   Curtain wall.

fausse braie   Low-walled outwork.

fieldstones   Naturally available rocks or small boulders.

forewalls   Additional defensive walls in front of the main defensive walls and towers.

fosse   Defensive ditch.

galleries   Passage, usually within a defensive wall, sometimes with embrasures.

glacis   Smooth, open slope leading up to the base of a fortified wall.

hoarding   Wooden structure in the form of a gallery mounted on top of, and ahead of, a defensive wall.

huchette   A form of machicolation above an entrance.

keep   Main tower of a fortified position (see also *donjon*).

machicolation   Overhanging structure on a tower or fortified wall, down which arrows could be shot or missiles dropped.

mahone   Local Genoese authorities in one of the Genoese colonial outposts.

merlons   Raised pieces of masonry forming a *crenellation*.

moat   Ditch or fosse forming an obstruction outside a defensive wall, sometimes but not necessarily filled with water.

portcullis   Grid-like gate, usually raised and lowered into position inside a gateway.

posterns   Small door or gate in the defences of a fortified position.

put-log   Holes in masonry into which supporting beams are thrust.

redoubt   Outwork of a fortified place.

salient towers   Towers thrust forwards from a fortified wall.

spur-castle   Castle built on a spur or promontory, usually on the side of a hill.

talus   Additional sloping front along the lower part of a wall and tower.

terrepleine   Open area on top of a rampart as an emplacement for cannon.

undercroft   Lowest chamber of a multi-storey building or structure.

ward   Open area surrounded by a curtain wall.

Index